C0-FQF-069

How to Talk Your Way to Success in Selling

Philip J. Koerper

PARKER PUBLISHING COMPANY, INC.
West Nyack, NY

© 1979 *by*
Parker Publishing Company, Inc.

West Nyack, N.Y.

All rights reserved. No part of this book may be reproduced in any form or by any means, without permission in writing from the publisher.

Reward Edition . . . . . . September 1980

Library of Congress Cataloging in Publication Data

Koerper, Philip J
How to talk your way to success in selling.

Includes index.
1. Selling. 2. Success. I. Title.
HF5438.25.K63 658.85 78-20854

Printed in the United States of America

Dedication

Dedicated to my wife, Virginia, without whose love, patience, and understanding, this book could have never been written.

HOW THIS BOOK CAN HELP YOU INCREASE YOUR SALES

This book gives you proven selling skills and techniques that will help you talk your way to increased sales and more money. It offers dramatic procedures and methods that you can put to use immediately.

Oversimplified, selling is taking a product or idea, developing a program for it, presenting it to a buyer who isn't necessarily interested in it, or doesn't think he wants it, or doesn't need it—and finally *talking him into buying it*, and making him feel happy that he did. The definition suggests that there are four areas involved in talking your way to a sale—*product, preparation, presentation*, and *persuasion*. While this book does deal with the first two, the emphasis is on the third and fourth; *presentation* and *persuasion*—where you make it or lose it.

When you enter the arena alone, nose to nose with the buyer, don't forget that he has the home-court advantage. Also, always remember that he, too, is a salesman, and his most formidable weapon is his ability and frequent eagerness to say "No." He will make it stick, too, unless you have some secret weapons of your own. You can be a walking encyclopedia of knowledge concerning the product you are selling, and you may come prepared with charts, plans, samples, and gimmicks—along with a lot of enthusiasm—but you'll never be a winner if you fall for the buyer's own sales pitch, or can't find a way to cut him off at the pass before he can say "No."

That is precisely what this book is about—to help you build your own arsenal of selling skills and techniques, and tell how you can successfully use and implement them. I make reference throughout the book to exciting procedures that have worked for me as well as other salespersons—not mere theoretical prattle, but techniques and ideas based on actual experience.

I tell how a floor covering salesman, by using the ego appeal technique, increased his sales volume in one city 50% in less than a year. You will learn how one insurance salesman used flexibility in planning to put himself in the Million Dollar Club. I relate how a real estate salesman used the twist technique to work his way to a $125,000 a year income bracket. These and many other techniques in this book will work for you, too, if you will but try them. I also give you systems, procedures, rules, and axioms to help you talk your way to successful selling.

This book stresses the importance of learning all you can about the strengths and weaknesses of your adversary, the buyer, before you enter the selling arena with him. It also illustrates how to use your own product knowledge and selling skills, and suggests vivid ways in which you can more effectively implement them in planning your work and working your plan.

I face head-on the problems and complaints that too often plague you: how to turn these negatives into positives; how to use them to talk your way to sales; how to avoid the dangers of the "Don't's" that too frequently muddy the presentation.

As the title suggests, one of the most powerful weapons you have is your ability to talk. This book goes further than that by emphasizing the importance of your knowing when *not* to talk: how to be a good listener; how to recognize the wisdom of silence.

This book gives you specific selling skills and techniques that you can use at the beginning of your sale—how to open; during your presentations—how to use your persuasion skills; and at the end, when the buyer begins to make waves and looks like he wants to back away—how to keep him from saying "No." I present a simple three-step formula that you can use effectively to talk your way to sales. Finally, the book tells you how to ask for the order.

Whenever I pick up a book on salesmanship, I always hope to find one selling skill or technique that will help me become a more productive salesman. If I do, the book more than pays for itself. I have used the direct how-to-do-it approach/because that is the language that we, as experienced salespersons, understand. You will find that I have eliminated the stalks, the chaff, the stems, the flowers, and the leaves/to get down to the nitty gritty—the kernel and the grain.

Philip J. Koerper

Acknowledgments

I acknowledge with warmest thanks the contributions of many salespersons—too numerous to mention by name—who willingly shared their experiences with me; the help of busy sales managers and other executives who devoted some of their valuable time to lend their expertise to this book; and finally, Sally Barringer, my "girl Friday," for her encouragement, helpful suggestions and ideas—and her incredible efficiency.

CONTENTS

1

USING KNOW-HOW TO TALK YOUR WAY TO SUCCESSFUL SELLING

Take a good look around you and ask yourself why is it that some are successful and make it big, while others struggle to eke out a mere existence? What are the ingredients that make for success or mediocrity—or even failure? What can a salesperson do to turn himself around from being an average performer, to become a top producer in his chosen field? What are the secrets of good salesmanship?

These questions have been asked many times by many people. Unfortunately, there are no magic formulas or wand-waving answers to any of them. There are many who tell you that if you work hard, put in long hours, and keep your personal batteries charged up by reading inspirational books success will eventually be your reward. I don't agree.

Perhaps mine is a contrary opinion, but it is dictated by over thirty years of experience and observation in the marketplace. Many of the highest paid salespersons I have known are not hard workers. They are painstaking and well-organized individuals, to be sure, but their success is attributable to how they work and what they do with the store of knowledge that is available, rather than how hard they work or how many hours they put in.

I have seen salespersons literally knock themselves out working long hard hours, but their efforts were helter-skelter. They were like squirrels running on a treadmill in a cage—getting nowhere. No, hard work alone is definitely not the panacea for a failure syndrome. For my money, I would rather take a slow, easy-going salesperson who has a lot of moxie, thinks straight, and uses proven skills and techniques in preference to a fast moving hard worker who is a textbook thinker and is short on imagination. You can be a lazy mover, but you'll never make it if you're a lazy thinker.

The difference can be summed up in one simple hyphenated word—know-how—which *Webster's New World Dictionary of the American Language,* Second College Edition defines as "knowledge of how to do something well." Pound this word into the inner cells of your brain. It is the very essence of good salesmanship.

USE PRODUCT KNOWLEDGE TO TALK YOUR WAY TO THE SALE

Experienced salespersons occasionally make a serious mistake in taking their product knowledge for granted. Never forget that excellence in product knowledge is the very first requisite for good salesmanship. You may be gifted with a glib tongue and come to your buyer well armed with plans for a sure-fire presentation, but if you are not completely familiar with your product and if you don't have quick information concerning it on the tip of your tongue, your sales plane will never get off the ground. Don't ever attempt to kid your buyer by trying to toe dance around the facts because of your inadequate knowledge of the product.

One of the sharpest buyers I ever knew once told me, "I can smell a salesman who is poorly equipped with facts about his product a mile away. He gets the axe damned quick. I can't afford to waste my time on him. I buy information as well as merchandise."

You'll bait your own trap if you try to talk your way to a sale by bluffing. It won't work. There is no substitute for product knowledge. Buyers aren't fools. The moment they get the feeling that you are evasive and unsure of yourself, they will put into motion their own tactics of diversion to completely disarm you and throw your presentation off the track. You then lose the ball and go on the defensive, a situation every salesperson must avoid at all costs. It becomes pickup time—the game is over.

The Importance of Having a Working Knowledge of Your Product

The significance of having good product knowledge is best evidenced by the fact that many large corporations spend hundreds of thousands of dollars annually to bring in their salespersons from all over the country to update them on the products they are selling. Time and experience have proven that this expenditure pays off. Why? Simply because their salespersons always know what they are talking about.

It is important that you recognize the fact that selling is not an exact science. There are too many variables and uncertainties involved. One thing you can count on, however, and that is that you will never make your way to the winner's platform if you don't have good solid product knowledge. Actually, it is the most effective selling tool you have at your disposal. Without it, you can forget your selling techniques and skills and all of the other elements necessary for good salesmanship—they will be like so much frosting without the cake.

I once had the occasion to know two salesmen who worked for a company that sells its products door-to-door. Both were neat in appearance, personable, and spoke well. There was one thing that differentiated them, however. Fred didn't have a solid knowledge of his products, while Solly was a fountain of information concerning them. Solly was better equipped to do a selling job.

When Fred moved to another city, Solly replaced him. There was little to choose between them at first, but then Solly's product knowledge began to show. Their sales records proved the point. I know, because in both instances my wife was the buyer—and *I* paid the bills.

Solly stayed on the territory only three years. On his last call he told one customer, "I wasn't at all happy with my income the first year, so I decided to do something about it, by mastering my products. In a year's time, my commissions increased better than 30%. The next year I kept getting increases, and well, not long ago I got a break and I've been tabbed for management. I hate to leave my route, but this is something I've wanted for a long time."

No doubt, there were other things that prompted his firm to move him to management, but there is no question that his thorough product knowledge played an important role in his promotion. It paid off for him not only in increased commissions, but as a stepping stone to a better job. When you take a personal inventory of your own product knowledge, how do you score yourself? If you are satisfied, that's just fine; but think carefully, because you might well be living in the rarified atmosphere of complacency. If your score is low, all I can say is that you are standing at home plate swinging with a broken bat. But don't let that discourage you, because it's never too late to get back to the drawing board and sharpen up your product knowledge skills. When you do this, you will be taking a major step toward starting to talk your way to successful selling.

Make Superiority in Product Knowledge Pay Off For You

I once watched Lee Trevino for two hours on a driving range, hitting irons to perfect his short game. It paid off for him in the tournament that followed. As a salesperson, you, likewise, can perfect your own selling capabilities and know-how by first *wanting* to master your skills, and then setting out to do something about it. The place to start is with the product you are selling. Increase your knowledge, and add strength to your sales efforts. The difference between superiority and mediocrity is often one word—*desire*. Trevino has it—so can you.

I had one assistant manager who was a one-time all-star football player from the South. Pete was as tough in the selling game as he was on the football field. Because of his superb product knowledge and know-how in the contract field, he earned the respect of architects, contractors, customers, and even our competitors. He set out to be a specialist and he attained his objective. When he said, "It is my opinion that . . . ," people paid close attention to his words because they had a ring of authority. In many instances his reputation paved the way for business that we would not otherwise have been able to touch. It paid off for Pete and for the company as well.

There are other ingredients that go into the mix for successful salesmanship, but being recognized for your expertise opens many doors that you might not otherwise be able to penetrate. This in itself is a positive benefit that comes only to the skilled.

Throughout the years, I have been amazed at the ingenuity and straight thinking of some of the salespersons I have met. I recall one named Harry Stanton who was a salesman for an office furniture manufacturer. He told me an interesting and pertinent success story. Early in his career, he learned that few in his business concerned themselves with mats under swivel chairs to protect floors. They were much too interested in selling office furniture, and left the floors for the customer to worry about. He decided to do something about it. He set out to become an expert on protective mats by learning all about the materials that were available so he could make specific recommendations. It wasn't long before the word got out and customers began to look to him for advice.

Harry explained, "I began to sell a lot of mats, but the real payoff was that I also got myself some new customers for office furniture, and that's where the money is. I increased my business each year over a fifteen year span and I'm sure those mats had a lot to do with it. Everybody's gotten into the act now, but I still continue to get calls. I guess it pays to be first with an idea when you are in a business as competitive as mine."

Harry and Pete found that by being well informed in a special field, they became experts, and people came knocking on their doors for help when they had a problem. You can do the same. It takes know-how along with determination and imagination.

How to Use The Technique of Dependency to Talk Your Way to Increased Sales

Only a few will ever become true "stars," but that certainly doesn't mean that all is lost for the rest of you. On the contrary, the opportunity to establish sound seller-buyer relationships that are mutually profitable is available to every salesperson. Always bear in mind that in addition to being a source of supply to your buyer, you are also an important provider of information. He has to depend on you for up-to-date data on new styles, changes in price structures, new products and innovations, etc. You need his business, but at the same time he needs the advice and knowledge that you can impart to him. Be a *consultant* to him, be his *teacher*—make him so dependent on you that you establish yourself as more than just another salesperson to him.

Actually, the technique of dependency—making the buyer depend on you—is one of those tools all salespersons can use, yet it frequently goes begging. You often get so carried away with your efforts to make a sale (because of what it means to you financially), that you forget the buyer is in business for one reason only—to make a profit.

To many buyers as well as consumers, buying can be a painful experience. When you consider the mind-muddling variety of types, patterns, shapes, colors, designs, selections, and mechanisms in almost everything that is being sold today, there is little wonder why so many approach buying with caution and concern.

Whether you are selling at the retail level to the ultimate consumer or at the wholesale level to the retailer, your effectiveness in talking your way to sales can well depend on what kind of a teacher or consultant you are. Buyers at all levels are literally screaming for help. Give it to them. They will benefit from it and so will you—through increased sales.

Jimmy Nelson, salesman for a wholesale hardware company, was transferred from a high dollar sales area to a low volume territory. His new territory had greater potential than his old one, but his predecessor had let it go to pot. Jimmy agreed to accept the challenge only with the understanding that he be paid a salary equivalent to the previous year, *plus* a bonus based on a percentage of increase in dollar volume in the new territory.

For two weeks prior to actually making calls, he devoted his entire time to gathering information from others in his company concerning each of his new accounts: personal information on the buyers, credit information, past sales, complaint patterns, etc. With this background of information, he selected thirty key outlet stores that he designated as his prime targets.

His approach to each buyer was simple: "If you will give me an opportunity to learn more about your business, I will *guarantee* that I can help you increase your turnover and develop greater profits." It is not surprising that almost two-thirds of his prime targets responded favorably.

Then he went to work, checking their stock control systems, storage methods, handling of merchandise, display, markups, and all other facets of each store operation. As a result of his on-the-spot appraisal, Jimmy was able to recommend and make changes which eventually helped to achieve his objective—more profit for the owner, and more money for himself. In several stores he was so highly thought of that no moves were made without consulting him first. His use of the technique of dependency began to pay off. He had made himself indispensable!

The bottom line of this case story is that Jimmy earned a bonus of $8,500 for his first year on the new territory. He combined his know-how with the technique of dependency to accomplish dramatic results.

I can't think of an area of selling where the technique of dependency is more relevant than in salesmanship at the consumer level. Most buyers, many of whom are women, are literally at the mercy of the salesperson. And yet, it seems that something has happened to retail selling. Perhaps this is another contrary opinion, but it is apparent to me that salesmanship at this level is slowly but surely becoming a lost art. To prove my point, go into almost any store, large or small, and try to find a salesperson who will really help you—one who will use the technique of dependency. Quite often, when you try to get help from some alleged salespersons, they always seem to be chatting with one another, or are preoccupied doing something else. Obviously there are exceptions, but they stand out like shining beacons in a storm of indifference.

I recently went to a department store to buy a certain make of transistor radio. The clerk (I refuse to prostitute the word *salesperson*) who waited on me was so disinterested and bored about the whole thing that I became exasperated, and walked out empty-handed. I returned the next day, hoping someone else would be there to help me. I lucked out. The irritator had gone to lunch.

In his stead was a saleslady who immediately put me at ease and was so adept at using the technique of dependency that she not only answered all my questions, but convinced me that I should buy the top grade of the brand I had in mind. I needed help; she had know-how as well as interest; my uncertainty turned to confidence in her, and she made the sale. I spent twice the amount of money I had anticipated because she did an excellent job of trading me up.

I doubt very much that she qualified as an expert on radios, but she certainly was a welcome source of information for me. As a result, she not only made a nice sale, but got a boost with her boss as well; I sought out the store manager afterward and complimented the saleslady on the manner in which she had handled herself.

Indifference is not exclusive to salesmanship at the consumer level. Some salespersons at the manufacturer and distributor levels have a lethargic attitude, and it is quite apparent that they are putting in time, waiting for their paychecks. It's little wonder that they are failures. If your buyer ever gets the feeling that you are disinterested in him or lackadaisical about your work, the "No sale" sign will quickly flash on his cash register. By all means, avoid such an attitude. *Make that buyer in front of you feel that he is the most important customer you have*, even though he knows better. Make him believe that your only concern is what is best for him. Educate him; help him in every way possible. Make yourself indispensable to him and you will be rewarded with orders. After all, isn't that what you are there for?

THE IMPORTANCE OF RECOGNIZING YOUR BUYER'S DEFENSES

When you enter the arena loaded with your weapons of product knowledge and secret plans for your assault on the buyer, never forget that he, likewise, has his own arsenal of defensive skills and techniques to offset yours. If you have done your homework properly, however, you have one decided advantage over him, and that is the element of *surprise*. You are on the offensive and call the shots, at least at the start of the encounter. You know what you are going to talk about—he doesn't. But don't let that make you over-confident—don't be smug about the situation. He knows exactly why you are there, that your real purpose in calling on him is to sell him and make money for yourself.

Actually, you are imposing on his valuable time for purely selfish reasons. You may have surprise on your side, but he knows that he doesn't have to buy from you. Therefore, I can't think of a worse approach for a salesperson to take than "You can't get along without this." He not only can, but rest assured that he will; should you be so rash as to try to pull that one on him. Even experienced salespersons are sometimes guilty of forgetting that buyers, for the most part, aren't stupid, and if they choose to do so, they will use every weapon at their disposal to bomb you out of the arena.

One very potent defense that the buyer has on his side is his *home court advantage*. He is accustomed to sparring with salespersons and he has his own bag of tricks designed to stop you before you even get started. Did it ever occur to you that on most calls you make you are actually barging in on the buyer, uninvited, trespassing on his property and his privacy, often at times when he doesn't want to talk to anyone? Seeing you walk through his door isn't necessarily happy time for him. It is little wonder, then, that he is quick to open his bag of tricks and go to work on you.

He usually starts in with little hand weapon tidbits such as:

1. "I have an important meeting, and can't talk to you right now;" or
2. "I am happy with my source of supply and don't want to make any changes;" or
3. "I'm overstocked right now;" or
4. "Business hasn't been too good lately;" or
5. "Your prices are too high."

You can go on and on, adding words and stanzas to this familiar refrain, but the tune is always the same. It becomes vitally important that you recognize these as buyer's defenses. Quite often he doesn't really mean what he is saying—it is just his way of using his home court advantage to get rid of you. Unless you are prepared to come up with some quick answers, however, you'll find yourself sitting in the popcorn machine. Techniques and skills that will help you deal with these problems will be presented in subsequent chapters.

You run into some rather strange situations with buyers. One, whom I'll never forget, was a man who used the *disappear technique* when he wanted to stymie a salesperson. If he felt that he was fighting a losing battle and the salesperson was getting the best of things, he always signalled to one of the girls in the office to call him for an "important telephone call." He immediately disappeared and with him went any chance for the salesperson to make a sale.

I had been forewarned, so when he pulled his disappearing act on me, I picked up my samples and followed him to the door of his office where I sat and outwaited him. Fortunately there aren't too many of this type of buyer. My purpose in telling you about this man is to show the extremes to which buyers will go to try to discourage you. If you learn to recognize their tricks and resistance techniques you will be better equipped to cope with them.

Take the time to put yourself in the buyer's shoes and then think of all the resistance barriers you would throw up if someone tried to sell you something. By doing this you will better understand what you are up against when you confront your own buyers.

Of all the defensive ploys ever employed by buyers, the one that can really frustrate a salesperson is the *clam up technique*. There is nothing more disconcerting than to have a buyer stand and look at you through beady eyes in complete silence. You make a suggestion that calls for a comment, and you don't get so much as a grunt in return. You ask a question and you get a blank stare.

Some buyers are masters in this kind of psychological warfare, and it takes a lot of guts to hang in there and keep talking. It becomes a waiting game on your part. Sometimes he will give in and finally respond to your questions. Sometimes he doesn't. As you go through the pages of this book we will go into skills and techniques that will help you deal with this kind of buyer and others who use variations of this technique.

Then there is the buyer who uses the *stall technique*. He makes you wait for him hoping you will go away. You can't afford to sit all day, so when time is running out, the smart thing to do is leave, but not before trying to set up an appointment with his secretary at a later date. With this type of buyer, making an appointment is the only possible way you can get to him. Don't waste your time trying to make "Cold" calls on some buyers. They'll see you only by appointment.

When all else fails him and he can't knock you out with the small weapons in his arsenal, he'll reach for the big one—his ability to say "No." An entire chapter is devoted to selling skills and techniques to help you keep him from using this weapon (Chapter 10).

Always respect your buyer as an individual, but also give him credit for having the know-how to resist anything and everything you carry in your own arsenal of selling weapons. Remember—he is also a salesman, trying to sell you on why he won't buy from you. He can be a powerful adversary, and if you recognize him as such, your chances for talking your way to successful sales are greatly enhanced. If you have your guard up, you are prepared to recognize and defend against his defensive maneuvers.

GET TO KNOW ALL YOU CAN ABOUT THE BUYER

Knowledge of your buyer is a close second to knowledge of your product. It is necessary that you keep yourself well informed concerning all aspects of his business if you expect to produce successful sales with him.

I recently asked a very well-known and successful insurance executive what, in his opinion, is the most important ingredient for successful salesmanship in his field. Without any hesitation he replied, "Knowing and understanding the needs of the client. You have to know about his business, his family situation, and what you can do to give him protection and peace of mind, which are basically the two products we are selling."

This may be another contrary opinion, but I suspect that most salespersons generally do an inadequate job of researching their customers to find out what makes them act the way they do. Unless you know all about your buyer, you are not going to be able to effectively use and implement what I call the skill of anticipation.

Profit from the analytical approach used by the United States Army. The *Staff Officer's Field Manual* goes into great detail to spell out the importance of knowing the enemy's capabilities before the field commander can reach a decision as to what line of action is to be taken. Football coaches go to great lengths to scout opposing teams, and from information that is compiled, set up their game plans for ensuing encounters.

In both cases, based on information that is available, they are in a position to anticipate what the opposition can be expected to do. The salesperson has to take the same approach concerning his buyer. You have to know what you can anticipate when you walk through his door. Throughout the years I knew many buyers whom I considered to be my friends, but I never entered their "Parlor" when I was selling without keeping a watchful eye for the "Web" that might snag my sales presentation.

Always remember that off the field you may be friends, but once you step into the arena with the buyer, he is your adversary. Don't get caught with your head in the sand. You either sell him or he sells you—it's that simple. The more you know about your buyer, the better your chances to talk your way into a successful sale. Information is available to you. All you have to do is take the time to look for it. There are three important areas that will help you: (1) evaluation reports; (2) information concerning the personal life of your buyer; and (3) basic differences in buyers.

How to Develop and Use Evaluation Reports

Simply stated, evaluation reports are a reconnaissance of your customer's business. By having in advance all pertinent information concerning your buyer, you will be in a position to establish your own game plan for each call. There may be other factors involved, but there are four things you must know about your buyer:

1. How important is he to your overall business?
2. What type of trade does he cater to?
3. What are his loyalties and buying habits?
4. Does he pay his bills?

How important is he to your overall business? How much time can you afford to spend with him? When you go fishing, always go where the big fish are biting, even though it may be more peaceful in the small ponds where the little fish repose. I have observed good salesmen wasting time on small accounts just to get out of the rat race and relax in an atmosphere of quiet friendliness. I used to have my own little haunts away from reality and pressure. I felt justified in goofing off because they were customers.

Fortunately, I got cured fairly early in my selling career. I had an appointment for a job take-off with a dealer in a nearby town, but got involved in a quiet game of gin rummy with one of my favorite "Hang out" accounts. We got so interested in the game, I forgot all about the time.

When I suddenly realized that the hour was late, I raced to the next town, only to learn that one of my competitors had beaten me to it—he was on the job! Fortunately for me, my competitor made the mistake of trying to high pressure the buyer into the order, and that cooled him off. After much sweating, I finally got the order. That gin rummy game almost cost me some fine business.

There is always a possibility that some of your small customers may grow to major proportions over the years, but usually the small ones remain small while the big ones grow bigger. Quit wasting time cooling your heels in your little hide-a-way haunts. It can get to be a bad habit. I think most of you know exactly what I am referring to.

Past sales records for each account become invaluable to you. The figures show trends in business and will help you to evaluate your own efforts. With this information, you are in a position to talk sensibly about his business with the buyer, and it will also tell you which of your customers calls for more concentrated time and effort. These records can be important weapons in your selling arsenal. Use them intelligently and frequently!

What type of trade does he cater to? An important part of the evaluation of your customer is a determination concerning the kind of business he is engaged in—the type of people he is selling. Salespersons are frequently guilty of trying to sell the wrong thing to the wrong buyer.

As a ladies apparel salesperson, you would be wasting your time trying to sell mini skirts to a store that caters to the retirement home set.

Since the whole reason for the buyer's purchasing anything from you is to make money for himself, be sure you sell him merchandise he can move. Never try to stick him with something you want to rid yourself of. If you con him into buying something he can't sell, he'll remind you of it every time he sees you.

A furniture manufacturer once had a promotion on some table lamps. At the time, colorful porcelain lamps were popular. One salesman, Joe Machele, decided he was going to win first prize in the promotion, which involved a trip for two to Hawaii, so he loaded every dealer in his territory with some of the worst looking lamps imaginable—mostly fruit and vegetable designed monstrosities. He got his trip to Hawaii, but he more than paid for it by having to listen to conversation about those lamps for months to come.

Joe's evaluation was poor, and he made a costly mistake. Those lamps would have sold in stores catering to lower income groups, but his was the carriage trade and there was no way that his dealers could do a job of merchandising them to their own customers. As a result, they just sat there as constant reminders of his bad judgment. Eventually they all were returned and sold at a substantial loss to a large discount house. Everbody lost, but Joe lost the most—the confidence of his customers.

What are his loyalties and buying habits? One cynical salesman once remarked, "the only thing that buyers are loyal to is the 'long green'." Perhaps there is some truth in this, but I contend that your buyer's loyalty to you is conditioned to a great degree by your own selling capabilities. Ask yourself what makes him want to buy from you or from somebody else. Is it price? Is it service? Is it quality? Is it, perhaps, salesmanship? I suspect, from general observation, that salesmanship is often the deciding factor. It is rather ego deflating to face up to the fact that someone may be outselling you. When that happens, who do you blame?

Buyer loyalty is something every salesperson strives for. One simple fact is too often overlooked, however. Loyalty must be *earned.* It isn't handed to you on a silver platter. Good salesmanship requires that you know who your loyal accounts are and which are the ones you can't count on. Armed with that information, you set up a program to keep your loyal buyers loyal and work on the others to come your way.

Never underestimate the importance of the buying habits of your buyers. Some buy only at set hours. Others will see you by appointment only. Some are "morning people" and are receptive only before noon, while others respond best in the afternoon—particularly after you have picked up the tab for their lunch.

Learn to know the idiosyncracies and habits of your buyers. This information can help you talk your way to more successful sales by developing and keeping loyal accounts.

Does he pay his bills? You may have a thorough knowledge of your product, give a good pitch to your buyer, and talk your way to a successful sale, but if he can't pay his bills, you are wasting your time. Past records showing credit information on each of your accounts are important guidelines to tell how far you can go in your selling efforts.

The very first trip I made into the territory was a real eye-opener for me on this subject. I called on a furniture store in a small community near a resort area. When I noted how depleted the floor covering inventory was, I went to work, using all my skills and techniques. I ended up with a sizable stock order. When I left the store and went on to my next call, I felt like striking up the band. Here was a real sleeper that had been waiting for some smart young salesperson to come along—namely myself.

My balloon was quickly deflated when my order hit the desk of the credit manager. He hit the ceiling! I was advised in no uncertain terms that the buyer was a no good so and so who didn't pay his bills and what did I mean by bringing in a big order from him? You know what that credit manager did? He tore up my beautiful order into little pieces and disdainfully tossed it into the wastebasket.

The moral to this story is that you must have credit information on each of your accounts. If you don't, you can get yourself in some embarrassing situations. After all, why go through all the motions of talking your way to a sale if you can't make delivery because the buyer can't pay the bill?

The Importance of Knowing All You Can About The Personal Life of Your Buyer

There is one thing that I have always noticed about successful salespersons. They carefully observe others who are proven successes to see what can be learned from them.

I recall one salesman, Morris Rinton, who represented a major appliance manufacturer, and was covering substantially the same territory I was assigned to at the time. Morris was a walking encyclopedia of information concerning his buyers, many of whom I also called on. I asked him one night when we were having dinner together in a hotel how he knew so much about the personal lives of his customers when he had, in fact, been on the territory such a relatively short time.

Morris answered, "Getting to know your man, his hobbies, his interests, his family, and that sort of thing, is one of the best selling tools I have. It's one of the first things I do when I am assigned to a new territory." He then went on to say that he even set out to learn the birthdates of his buyers and had special cards printed to express his best wishes, and also thank them for their business. When I asked him if this had been worthwhile, he very quickly replied, "You better believe it!"

I didn't go so far as to send out birthday cards, but I did pull a page from the experience of this man and set up a card file in my desk, which I called my personality file. Your credit department and past records give you information on the buyer's business, but it's up to you to find out all you can about his personal life. My own card file was quite simple. I recommend that you establish one for your own use. There are only two things you need to know about your buyer's personal life:

1. First of all, if he is married; but more importantly, if he has children? Then, what are the children's interests and hobbies?

2. Secondly, what are his own outside interests?

Most people live through the eyes of their children, and your buyers are no exception. In some thirty years in selling I must have attended at least thirty high school football, basketball, and Little League baseball games with buyers whose sons were playing. Do you think this interest on my part hurt me or helped me the next time I called on them with samples under my arm? I have even suffered through several evenings of junior ballet performances and piano recitals, watching some buyer's "Little Emily" do her stuff; but my order book didn't suffer because of it. You have to be prepared to pull out all stops when you are selling.

Rule: If it doesn't harm anyone in any way; if it isn't deceitful or dishonest; if it is beneficial to someone—use it!

If you have never had some particular individual or circumstance that was bugging you, all I can say is that you are indeed fortunate. I was discussing this subject with Rich Stacey, a successful sports clothing salesman. He related a very interesting personal experience to me. Stacey told me, "When I started out selling I had one account who gave me a lot of trouble. I just wasn't able to get along with the buyer. Our sales were slipping, and I was determined to find some way to get to this buyer. I finally made it. I accidentally learned that his son was a Little Leaguer, so I started to talk baseball. He warmed up just a little but it wasn't until I decided to part with a baseball that had the signatures of a World Series Championship baseball team on it, that things really changed. Our relationship improved and within six months I had almost doubled my dollar volume with him. All because I gave his son that little old baseball."

This salesman successfully applied the appeal to the heart technique.

No one was harmed; there was no deceit or dishonesty on his part, and everybody benefited. The buyer felt more friendly toward him; he increased his business; and the kid received the adulation of his team because he owned that baseball.

I cite this experience because it shows how important small things can become in the fast pace of today's business. It also proves how worthwhile having personal information concerning your buyer can be. You have to use all the know-how and help you can get to talk your way to successful sales.

How To Cope With Basic Differences in Buyers

It is extremely difficult to try to establish standards for reading your buyers' minds, because you are dealing with one of the uncertainties of selling. They just don't act and react the same. Sometimes this is due to the salesperson himself while other times it is because of the buyer. I certainly don't intend to get involved in any discussions on psychology, but I do submit that we have to take into consideration the fact that people are different and don't all think alike.

In classifying buyers, I find that they fall into three general categories:

1. Those that are afraid to be sold.
2. Those that want to be sold.
3. Those that resist being sold.

What to do with the buyer who is afraid. This may be another contrary opinion because you might not agree that there are such buyers. However, I have had serious discussions with some rather important buyers who confessed to me that they are afraid whenever a salesperson approaches them. Actually, they are not afraid of the salesperson—they are, for the most part, afraid of themselves. Usually this fear is based on their own ineptitude and lack of self-confidence.

Such a buyer has only one line of defense, and that is a big "No" to everything the salesperson throws at him. He literally cringes when a salesperson makes a good presentation because he knows that he is a pushover for a good sales pitch. His inventory is usually full of mistakes he made in the past, because he was a patsy for some fast-talking salesman. As a result, he has thrown a mental iron curtain around himself.

How do you cope with such a buyer? If you are a pressure salesperson and try to pour it on him—forget it! He will freeze up in his tracks, say "No," and really mean it. His fear becomes suspicion and he will turn you down flat. There is only one way to handle a buyer who is afraid of himself, and that is to give him confidence. You have to make him feel that you are not only his consultant, but his confidant as well. Let him know that you are looking out for his interests and that you will protect him from your competitors who are bent upon taking his money away from him.

A successful specialty floor covering dealer I once called on fell in this category. Because of his large volume of business, salespersons from all manufacturers beat a path to his door. But, most of them used the wrong approach on him. He had been born in the old country and still retained the characteristics of his homeland—he was sensitive as well as successful.

Believe it or not, it was one of my competitors who taught me how to sell him. I wasn't doing too well with this customer, so I began to watch the salesman who was getting the lion's share of his business. I cased the joint, as it were, and put in my own stakeout. One day Joe Hertel, my competitor, walked in with samples under one arm and a paper sack filled with doughnuts under the other. He and the buyer then sat in the office and had a nice little coffee klatch before the samples and order book came out.

I subsequently started to do the same, and more and more of my products began to show up on his sales floor. Maybe I had fresher doughnuts than my competitor, but whatever the reason, the results were what interested me most. The technique of protection went to work for me. Just sitting and having coffee and doughnuts with him made that buyer feel *safe*. Anyone who was willing to do that wouldn't take advantage of him. His fear turned to confidence; his confidence turned to interest; and his interest turned to orders. Within four months I enjoyed a thirty percent increase in dollar sales with him. It's surprising what a couple of doughnuts and a little patience can do for you!

Bill Mohler, manufacturer's representative, sold two of his products, builder's hardware and decorative hardware, to Mr. Anderson, owner and buyer of the largest building material outlet in his entire territory. He enjoyed a fine business with this firm, but so did all of his competitors. Anderson bought from everybody. He was a salesman's dream.

One day Anderson complained to Bill that he wasn't making any money in his builder's hardware department.

Bill said, "No wonder. You have too much inventory: a lot of duplication; a whole warehouse full of dead stock; and poor stock records. Put a moratorium on all buying until you get the situation straightened up. Mark down all of your dead stock and move it out. Once you've cleaned house, then put in a tight stock control system."

He continued, "Anderson, your biggest problem is you want to be a nice guy, so you buy from every salesman that comes along. Your inventory looks like a salesman's smorgasbord. What you need is protection—from yourself."

Anderson did what Bill suggested and put up the "No buy" sign for that department. Of course it backfired on Bill, because he, along with all other salespersons, wrote no business for a long period. After about ten months when things got cleared out, Bill had an inside track for future business because he had the courage to tell Anderson he needed protection. When it came time to put in new inventory, Bill's products got excellent representation. At the end of the first year of business on the new basis, Bill's commissions on this one account increased to $3,000. This was three times the amount of any previous year. Through the use of the technique of protection, Bill had a happy customer who was making money—but so was Bill Mohler! And, he had the assurance of continued good business in the years ahead.

It's not always easy to find the exact formula that will bring the fearful buyer around, but if you look hard enough and have the determination, you will find it. What he really wants and needs is protection—from himself and from unscrupulous salespersons. Use your own technique of protection to release him from all fears and doubts concerning your intentions with him.

How to handle the buyer who wants to be sold. This is an entirely different individual from the one who is afraid. Fortunately, most buyers fall in this category. Please let me make it clear that when I say they want to be sold, they respond only to good salesmanship. They are not about to just roll over and play dead to anyone who comes along with a briefcase and a bunch of samples. Many of these buyers are tough and they are difficult to sell. They have little respect for a salesman who doesn't have good product knowledge and know-how, or isn't well prepared to give a good presentation. They will react favorably only to a salesperson who is confident and will stand up to them nose to nose. Let the timid soul beware! These buyers resent weak-kneed salespersons who don't know what they are talking about. It is indeed fortunate that most buyers actually want to be sold, since it means that the salesperson who has good product knowledge and know-how can, in most cases, sell them. Subsequent chapters tell how the use of specific selling skills and techniques will enable alert salespersons to talk their way to successful sales with these buyers.

What to do with the buyer who resists being sold. Some buyers just don't like salespersons and do everything they can to give them a bad time. They usually pride themselves on having a reputation for being tough, and consider their time well spent if they can make a salesperson's life miserable. They are often masters at baiting the salesperson; leading him on, making him think he will write an order, and then lowering the boom on him. They may really want or need the merchandise you are trying to sell them, but they take a diabolical delight in saying something like, "I can use this. I'll phone the order in this afternoon." They refuse to give an order to any salesperson, even though they do business with his firm. They want to deal with the manager by phone. All the salesperson is good for is to handle complaints. Sound familiar?

Fortunately, this type of buyer is in the minority, but they can control a large volume of business, so they must be coped with. They are a challenge to any red-blooded salesperson. It's easy to say, "Oh well, as long as I get the business, I don't care if I don't write the order," but that's not the way to develop increased sales. I have run across a few of these buyers in my time, and in almost every instance found that they were once salespersons themselves. They apparently couldn't cut it in the selling game, so they have a built-in resentment toward salespersons who are successful. There is only one way to handle this sort of buyer and that is to resort to the technique of flattery.

Your approach should be along the following lines:

1. "You were a successful salesperson once yourself, so there isn't anything I tell you that you don't already know."
2. "If you were still selling, how would you present this to the buyer?"
3. "I understand you used to sell. Could you give me some advice or suggestions as to how I should go about selling this?"

When I was working a large metropolitan area, I had a buyer of this type who really used to burn me. The minute he saw me, he yelled to the girls in the office and asked, "Do we have any complaints?" When the answer was "No", that signalled the end of my call on him. If I tried to show him something like a new series of patterns he would reply, "I'll be dropping by the mart this afternoon. I'll take a look at them then," or "I'm too busy right now," both of which, translated into plain English, meant "Get the hell out of here." Although this account gave us considerable business, I never wrote an order there. I even had the experience of sitting in his office and listening to him while he telephoned an order, instead of giving me the satisfaction of writing it. After getting pushed around once each week for almost six months, I decided to take a straight approach, using four little words that worked almost like magic—*I have a problem*. Here I was giving him an opportunity to show me how good he was, so his immediate reaction was to want to help me. He couldn't resist asking what my problem was. It usually involved new patterns, and I enlisted his help in deciding which colors would be the best sellers. He would then proceed to pick the patterns he, himself, would buy, thereby putting himself in a position where he couldn't refuse to give me the order. Those four words marked the beginning of a better personal relationship with the buyer, but more importantly, signalled the start of a steady increase in volume for me.

Contrary to an old cliché, flattery does get you somewhere!

2

HOW TO GET THE SALE OFF ON THE RIGHT FOOT

Someone once said that we all start to die the minute we are born. It is likewise true that the salesperson starts to close or lose the sale the moment he steps into the arena with the buyer. When you are fortified with good product knowledge, have carefully planned your presentation, and are equipped with timetested skills and techniques, chances are good that you will be able to talk your way to positive results in a high percentage of cases, provided you get things off on the right foot.

The beginning—getting out of the starting blocks—is frequently a very difficult time for many salespersons. They sometimes lose the sale even before they start to talk. They confront the buyer with a bad case of jitters, or they don't have the faintest conception of what they are going to say to start their conversation. As a result, the buyer's first impression is not good—which is an unlikely basis on which to build a successful sale.

There is nothing unusual about being apprehensive and somewhat nervous when you approach your buyer. It only proves that you are human. Some famous actors even admit to being nauseated at times before the curtain goes up; but once they are on stage, they are relaxed and confident.

Have you ever been at a baseball game, observed a relief pitcher coming to the mound, and closely followed his procedure? With the bases loaded, no outs, and the score tied, his stomach is undoubtedly full of butterflies as he slowly walks from the bullpen. But once he steps on the mound, he confidently begins a three-step routine; (1) the warm-up; (2) the windup; and (3) the pitch. He doesn't stand up there and immediately start throwing to the batter. He first takes eight or ten warm-up tosses to get himself set and loose for the windup and pitch. As a salesperson, you can learn a great deal from the baseball pitcher and apply it to your own selling skills. Develop your own system of *warm-up, windup, and pitch*.

HOW TO APPROACH YOUR ADVERSARY—THE BUYER (the warm-up)

Your first few seconds with the buyer can have a profound effect on the end result of your selling effort. You can't start out by throwing your sales pitch at the buyer the moment you see him. He has a built-in resentment against any salesperson who walks in and figuratively grabs him by the arm and starts to give the old one-two. You have to feel your way and warm-up before you get down to business. You not only have to warm-up to get yourself loose, but of equal importance, you have to get the buyer loose, so he will be receptive when you make your first move.

There are two "road blocks," times when the buyer's resistance is the greatest. One is at the very beginning, when you first approach him, while the other is at the very end, when you try to close your sale. It is when the red flag is up that you must exercise extreme caution, or you might blow your sale.

At one end of the selling spectrum is the high pressure artist who comes at the buyer like King Kong and tries to overwhelm him, while at the other end is the reluctant milquetoast who isn't sure of himself and is afraid to be decisive. Both of these approaches, instead of loosening up the buyer, will have just the opposite effect on him. He tightens up and loses his receptivity; and his only thoughts are how to get rid of these intruders on his time. Somewhere between these two extremes is the ideal appraoch to the buyer—one that will cause him to lower his guard.

These time-tested openings will help you warm up your buyer and knock down his walls of resistance:

1. *"I'm glad I caught you in. I have something I am sure you will be interested in."* (You immediately pique his interest.)
2. *"I know you are a busy person, but if you will spend just five minutes of your time with me, it will prove to be worthwhile and profitable for you."* (When you talk about profit to the buyer, you are singing his favorite song.)
3. *"You are also in the selling business. I have something here that is right down your alley."* (He becomes receptive because he likes the idea of talking to you on a salesperson to salesperson basis.)
4. *"If you have a couple of moments, I would like to get your opinion on something."* (Of course he will give you some time—you have just touched his ego button.)
5. *"Your friend, Jim Bowers, suggested that I call on you to show you. . . . "* (He'll be curious to learn why his good friend sent you to him.)
6. *"That was quite a game Saturday. Our team sure did clobber them."* (When you know of your buyer's interest in sports, an opening like this can't miss.)

7. *"How did your son make out with his state bar exam?"* (You warm your buyer up instantly when you show an interest in his family.)
8. *"I have something here that is an exclusive item."* (The word exclusive is an instant attention-getter.)
9. *"This is made to order for your trade."* (His curiosity will make him want to know why.)

Use these approaches and develop others of your own, and you will be well equipped to open with the buyer. You can count on one thing. If you don't anticipate what you are going to say and if you fumble the ball at the outset, there isn't anyone around to read your rights to you. The buyer becomes your judge, jury, jailer, and executioner.

USE YOUR HANDS TO TALK YOUR WAY TO SALES (the windup)

Following the warm-up, you must convey to your buyer the fact that you are there to sell and your call is not merely to promote public relations.

I recall one salesman in my office who turned in very few trunk sales and I wondered why. A trip in the field with him quickly disclosed the reason. He walked into every store empty handed—no samples, no sales case. In fact, one buyer, when he saw him approaching his office even remarked, "Here comes my favorite good will man." And why shouldn't the buyer think that? My salesman didn't give any outward impression that he had come to sell, his hands full of nothing but air.

I told him, following our call on that buyer which was pleasant, but fruitless, "We are not in business just to develop good will. That doesn't pay for the rent and taxes. We are salesmen—we are out to make sales, not win popularity contests." I am sure that his customers were subsequently surprised when he walked in laden with his selling case and samples, but his orders proved that he had more than just good will to sell.

The use of hands approach of some door-to-door salespersons is magnificent. You open the door and what happens? A hand reaches out with some small item in it. What do you do? You take it in your own hand, of course. From that point on, you as the buyer may not necessarily feel obligated to buy something, but it is a proven fact that you become receptive to his sales pitch. It is a time-tested technique—get the customer into the act.

I shall never forget the first time I saw a yo-yo. My wife and I were in a toy store buying Christmas presents when a young man came in manipulating a roundlike object on the end of a string. Everyone in the store watched him, including the buyer-owner who exclaimed, "I don't know what it is or how much it costs, but how soon can you ship me twelve dozen of those contraptions?"

By using his hands and demonstrating what his product could do, the salesman made a nice sale. Had he walked into the store with a picture of his yo-yo, or carried it in his briefcase and just shown it to the buyer, it is questionable whether he would have written such a large order. He used his hands to talk his way into a good sale. He knew how to use the technique of demonstration.

Not everything can be put on the end of a string and manipulated like a yo-yo, but there are ways in which you can use your hands to show many things about your own product, such as smoothness to the touch, flexibility, hardness, softness, thickness, durability, texture, etc. The lesson you can learn from the door-to-door salesman and the yo-yo salesman is the wisdom of having *something* in your hand when you greet the buyer, preferably something that you can place in his hands. If you are selling carpets, hand him the sample and let him feel the quality; if you are selling shoes, let him feel the smoothness of the leather.

It is extremely important that you give the buyer a strong first impression that you came to sell. To help you toward that end always be mindful of the following **rule**: never come through a buyer's door empty handed. Always carry a briefcase, samples, or other tools of your business.

USE PROVEN SELLING TECHNIQUES TO START YOUR WAY TO THE SALE (the pitch)

After the warm-up and windup are completed, you now come to that "moment of truth" when you start your sales presentation. It would be simple to talk in generalities and do a lot of theorizing on this subject, but I prefer the realistic approach—time-tested skills and techniuqes that have worked effectively for others, and can work for you, if you will but only use them.

How to Make The Ego Appeal Technique Work For You.

If I were asked to single out the one selling technique that stands out above all others for effectiveness and universal application, I would choose the ego appeal technique—the use of flattery—gratifying the buyer's vanity, making him feel important. It makes little difference what you are selling or to whom you are selling it. It is a rare circumstance when a buyer will not respond positively to an appeal to his ego, which often has very sensitive nerve endings.

In the first chapter I told of a personal experience in which I used flattery to get to a buyer who resisted being sold. The ego appeal will work on all buyers, because they have one thing in common—they are human beings. There are a number of catch phrases you can use to send your own buyers on an ego trip:

1. "How do you feel regarding. . . . ?"
2. "Do you consider this to be a good item?"
3. "I wish I had more buyers like you."
4. "It's always a pleasure to sit down and talk with you."

5. "You have the nicest looking store in my whole territory."
6. "What would you do if you were in my shoes?"
7. "Could I ask you a question?"
8. "I respect your opinion, so I will be guided by what you say."
9. "You have a knack of always coming up with the right answers."
10. "You have been successful where others fail. What is your secret?"

Significantly, there is one word that appears in each of these phrases—**you**. When you use the ego appeal technique you are talking about a very important person—the buyer himself. It not only flatters him, but also gives you an opportunity to learn his viewpoint on the subject at hand. Entire books have been written about ego—it is unquestionably a compelling human impulse. A smart salesperson can use this knowledge to good advantage.

Years ago, Sandy Sanderson, one of my fellow salesmen, related an interesting and pertinent experience. He told me, "I have two dealers in this town up north. They do all of the floor covering business in the area. Jones was giving us almost one hundred percent of his business, but I wasn't getting more than ten percent of Smith's. The trouble was that Smith did twice the overall volume of Jones.

"I discussed this with Al Cutler, my wholesaler salesman, and we both agreed that something was gnawing at old man Smith that kept him from buying more from us, but we couldn't figure out what it was. He tipped me off one day when I was showing him a new line of patterns. He gave the samples a cursory glance and then rather caustically exclaimed, 'I suppose your friend Jones already bought some of these. Naturally, you always call on him first when you come to town.'

"So that was it! We had stepped on his ego and hurt him. He resented the fact that he was our second call and not the first. After all, he, and everyone else, knew that he was by far the largest dealer in town! I quickly went into a huddle with my wholesaler salesman and from that point on we both made Smith our first stop when we hit town. Furthermore, we made sure that he knew it. You wouldn't believe it, but within nine months we were getting almost forty percent of Smith's business—meanwhile keeping our one hundred percent status with Jones, who didn't care who we called on first."

Ridiculous, you say? Not at all. This case example only shows how powerful a force man's ego can be, and how small, insignificant things can often make the difference between getting business or losing it. No one will ever be able to convince Sandy that the ego appeal technique doesn't work. All it did for him was to increase his dollar volume in that town by almost fifty percent in less than a year!

I once called on a buyer who considered himself quite a Beau Brummel. Only one word could describe his choice of clothes—awful. Everybody talked about it behind his back, but no one dared face him with the facts because he was an important customer. He bought from everybody. He was loyal to no one, except himself. He purchased some from us, but I seemed to be butting my head against a wall trying to better our position with him. Then, I decided I had nothing to lose if I tried the ego appeal approach on him.

One day I asked, "Who's your tailor, Harry? You sure do have class." His reaction was almost instantaneous—increased buying from me, the thing that really counted. Every time I called on Harry, he had on a different outfit, one just as bad as the other. He was strictly a nut on clothes and spent a fortune on them. He frequently asked me, "How do you like these new threads? Feel the cloth." Of course, I always painted a picture of being envious, even though I thought what he was wearing looked like something that came off the rack at a church rummage sale. I didn't mind it at all, however, because we were getting more and more business from him.

Little things, but extremely important things! Keep your eyes and ears open for opportunities to use the ego appeal technique. It will pay off for you in increased sales.

Follow this **rule:** make it a point on every call to say something that will appeal to your buyer's ego.

Use The Process of Elimination Technique For Positive Results

This is another technique that works because it involves another human characteristic—indecision.

My wife tells me that most women go shopping for clothes in pairs. They want a lady friend along to help reach decisions. Have you ever watched a group of people in a restaurant trying to make up their minds what to order? They do a lot of eliminating, but they have a difficult time reaching a final decision. When the head waiter suggests a certain item, there is an air of relief and they are quick to respond because someone has made up their minds for them. Buyers are no different.

I was once in a men's clothing store and watched a young salesman use the process of elimination technique to perfection. He was selling neckties, and had them spread all over a counter in front of the man who was obviously the buyer. He then started to remove certain ties saying, "These colors won't sell for you; you already have some similar to these; these are too expensive for your trade; etc." until finally, when half of the ties were removed, he continued, "Now *these* will be good numbers for you." The buyer looked at the remaining ties on the counter and said, "Fine, send me six of each."

The buyer departed and while the salesman was writing the order, I walked up to him, introduced myself and said, "I am a salesman myself. I admired the technique you used to make that sale."

He smiled, introduced himself as Paul Bremmer and responded, "Oh, it always works for me. I lay out twice the amount I expect to sell, and then start knocking and eliminating 'till I get down to where I want to be. I include some real dogs just to make the rest of my ties look good. The buyer always agrees, of course, so it's an easy way to get an order."

Knocking and eliminating. Everytime I go into a store to buy a necktie, I think of Paul. He used the process of elimination technique with great finesse and expertise. He knew exactly what he was going to do before he walked into that store.

A similar case involves a wholesaler salesman—one of the best in the business. Bert was an expert in using specific selling skills, including the process of elimination technique. I ran across him in a dealer's store one day just as he was starting to make his pitch on a new line of seven colors in vinyl sheet goods. Not wanting to disturb him, I backed off and sat down, just near enough, however, so I could listen in and possibly learn something from him. He spread all seven 18 x 18 inch samples along the floor. The buyer took a fast look at them and exclaimed, "They're nice patterns, but. . . . "

Bert interrupted him before he had a chance to finish, "Of course, you wouldn't want to put in the whole line. For example, this one is too similar to that pattern you have in stock behind you." He picked up the sample and continued, "This one has too much blue, which isn't a good seller right now."

The buyer agreed as Bert picked up that sample, leaving five on the floor. The buyer then said, pointing to one of them, "I just don't care for that color combination." Bert agreed, so he picked up that sample, leaving four.

He pointed to one of the four and said, "This one is a good bathroom pattern so you'll want just a small roll. I suggest large rolls for the others because they are hot numbers." The buyer commented, "I'm a little overstocked right now, so. . . . " Bert quickly responded. "They won't be in for several weeks. Suppose I put you down for shipment on the fifteenth of next month."

What could the buyer say, but, "Well, okay. I guess I better have them. The fifteenth will be fine."

Great salesmanship! The use of this technique will get orders for you. It is one of the best ways you have to get the buyer into the act and at the same time help him make up his mind. If the necktie salesman and Bert had gone for the whole works, they might have lost it all. They deliberately set out to settle for less and the buyers were also willing to settle for less. The important thing is that in both cases they bought—and that's what it's all about.

Earlier in this book I mentioned Rich Stacey, a sports clothes salesman, who got his foot in the door with one buyer by giving his son a baseball.

I asked Stacey if he ever used the process of elimination technique and told him how salesmen in my own company had effectively used it.

His reply was, "I guess that's like what I call the reverse English technique—start out first by showing the buyer what he doesn't want to buy and then let him pick out what he's going to buy. I used to stumble along just trying to sell our goods and was doing fairly well for myself, but nothing big—made myself about $12,000 a year, which wasn't too bad in those days in the mid sixties.

"One of the old timers in the firm went back to his home town to open up a haberdashery store, but before he left, he tipped me off on how to really sell. Among other things, he recommended the reverse English technique to me and I started to use it right off the bat. It was probably the best advice I ever received.

"I can't tell you exactly how much my sales increased each year in the intervening years, but I do know that in five years' time I was making $27,000. We did add a few items to our line, but I know I never would have come close to my present income had my old friend not tipped me off on how to use the reverse English technique.

"A buyer is like everyone else. He really wants help. When you tell him he shouldn't buy something your are selling, you arouse his interest and he becomes receptive to what you *want* to sell him. This is a sure-fire technique and works every time. It sure worked for me!"

How The Dramatization-Absorption Technique Will Get Results For You

From a strictly technical point of view, the film "High Noon" was one of the best motion pictures ever produced. It was a masterpiece of unity in time, place, and action. If you saw the picture, you will recall that there wasn't a single moment in which the viewer wasn't on edge—completely absorbed in the dramatic development of the plot. As the clock ticked off the minutes, the viewer was made to "feel" the mounting tension until the very climax itself.

At this point you are probably wondering what "High Noon" has to do with salesmanship. Actually nothing, except for the fact that in this picture we see in action a selling skill that has been used by many successful salespersons—the dramatization-absorption technique, or, keeping your buyer's interest at such a high level that he literally becomes absorbed by the dramatization you give your product. Through the use of a dramatic straight line approach, never wandering from your main plot, you hold the buyer's interest and keep him from reaching for his arsenal of defensive weapons. In other words, you not only have to *get* the buyer's attention—you must *keep* it. That's one of the secrets of good salesmanship.

You might say, "that's fine for some, but mine is not the kind of product I can dramatize." Are you so sure of that? Colonel Sanders, at an age when most men are retired from active business, entered a highly competitive field and achieved outstanding success. He set out to accomplish two things: (1) to develop a quality product at a low cost to the consumer, and (2) to dramatize and glamorize chicken, and make people want to eat his particular brand. He succeeded on both counts, and the big buckets turning on the roofs of small buildings throughout the world are witness to the American system of private free enterprise at work.

Bill Crawford, drapery salesman introducing a new type of fire-resistant fabric, used the dramatization-absorption technique to make sales. The first thing Bill did when he met the buyer was to hand him a sample to let him feel the material so he would know there was nothing unusual about it. Then he took the sample and, holding a corner in his left hand, let it dangle. He lighted his cigarette lighter and held the flame under the lower corner. The buyer became completely absorbed, expecting the fabric to burst out in flames. It didn't—there was only a slight scorching where the flame came in direct contact with it. By a dramatic demonstration, the salesman showed that his material was in fact fire-resistant. How much more effective than merely *telling* the buyer about it!

Factory representatives often get themselves in a box by taking on too many lines. As a result, they dilute their efforts on any one individual item they represent. Things become complicated.

Jake Cooper, a salesman working for a multiple distributor, sold everything from automobile tires, radios, and electrical appliances to sundries and furniture. His was a case of too much diversification. All were profitable lines, but he couldn't give a fair shot to any of them because he just didn't have the time.

It was after he had eliminated over fifty percent of the items he had been selling that he became a specialist in his field. He was able to concentrate on what he was selling and dramatize his products so he could keep his buyers completely absorbed in them. The first year his income was a stand-off with the previous year. The following year Jake had an increase in commissions of 17%—on fewer products and fewer customers than he had when he was covering the whole line.

I strongly urge you to take a good look at the products you represent and delete those that are taking time but giving you little return. Do the same thing Jake did. Specialization is the only avenue through which you can successfully implement and use the dramatization-absorbtion technique.

The dramatization-absorption technique is frequently used in TV commercials. You see a traveling bag sitting in the center of a highway and a truck comes along at high speed and knocks it into the bushes. An examination shows there was no significant damage to the case from the impact. A watch is dropped from an airplane and when it is picked up, it is still ticking. There are other commercials that use this technique, and they all have one thing in common—they sell by dramatic demonstration instead of merely showing the product and talking about it.

Whatever you are selling, try to find something in it or about it that you can use to dramatize your presentation. It is when you get the buyer fully absorbed in what you are telling him, that you are on your way to a sale. Remember "High Noon."

How To Use The Give Him Something Extra Technique

When you are selling in a highly competitive field, you have to constantly think of ways to keep ahead of "the other guys." Frequently, there is very little difference between your product and those of your competitors—so you have to dig deep into your own bag of techniques to convince the buyer that he should buy from you. One route to take is to give him something extra—perhaps something that your competitors haven't thought of.

I know the significance of using the give him something extra technique, because I spent my entire selling career in the highly competitive floor covering business. Our quality, good name, and advertising were all valuable assets, but often, when we stepped into the selling arena, something extra was needed to push the buyer into a sale.

I recall one hospital job involving a large amount of vinyl asbestos tile. It was a nice order and all of our competitors as well as we ourselves were after the job. The architect's specification called for a solid floor of one color of marbelized tile, something that all manufacturers produced.

When things looked bad for us because we were not competitive pricewise, one of our contract salesmen went with his dealer to the hospital superintendent and suggested a single row on a contrasting color of tile to run down the center of each corridor. This would provide a traffic direction marker and would also enhance the beauty of the corridor by giving it a "customized" look—something special—at no extra cost.

Our flooring contractor got the order and our tile went on the job. On the basis of price alone, we could have lost the job, but by using the give him something extra technique, our salesman added a sizable number of dollars to our overall volume.

I asked an industrial and commercial real estate salesman what he attributed his success to. He told me, "That's a tough one to answer. Actually, I can't think of anything specific—there's just a combination of ideas I use to make my sales. There is one thing, however, that probably could be called my ace in the hole. Whenever I have a prospective customer, I survey the area I think he is interested in and try to pick a prestigious spot where well-known companies are situated. When my client learns that he will have important neighbors, his interest always mounts. It makes a whale of a lot of difference. It's a plus that often puts over the deal for me."

Do you recognize the ego appeal technique at work here along with the give him something extra technique? This salesman wasn't just selling empty lots and buildings. He was also selling prestige—that something extra for the buyer. This is an interesting case example because it demonstrates how combinations of selling skills can be used to talk your way to sales.

The fact that Henry Failing had made a number of successful closings during the previous year was indicated when he said his sales amounted to over $4,500,000. I have never known too much about real estate sales, but others in the field tell me Failing had to gross at least $150,000. Using the ego appeal technique and the give them something extra technique certainly paid off for him.

The give them something extra technique can be used in every line of business. Cereal manufacturers often include something extra in their packages. Resort hotels that place flowers or a bowl of fruit in each room daily, find that this pays off. Airlines, by offering free meals, drew many train customers who resented the high cost of eating in diners. Salespersons can also find many ways to implement the use of this technique.

Jack, a salesman-driver for a water bottle company used the give them something extra technique to increase his bonus payments. One day, one of his customers complained that it was difficult to lift the heavy bottles onto the dispenser to replace the empties. This gave Jack an idea, and he made it a point to talk to each customer on his route about this matter. Some men could easily handle the bottles themselves—many couldn't. For the latter he agreed to drop by once each week to replace the bottles that had been emptied.

Customers were so pleased with this something extra that they told their friends, and soon Jack had built up quite a clientele. An additional bonus of $525 certainly made his efforts worthwhile.

The give him something extra technique can be extremely effective in selling at the store-consumer level. The cosmetic section in any department store is a prime example. I recently went to one to buy some perfume for my wife. There were three salesladies but two were taking inventory and were too preoccupied to help me, and the third had just started to wait on a lady customer. While waiting, I listened to their conversation. It went something like this:

The lady said, "I would like a lipstick in that brand. Do you have it in cherry red?" She pointed to a display on the counter.

"Yes we do," the saleslady replied, opening a drawer under the counter from which she removed a small box. She went on, "Will there be anything else?"

"No, I think not," was the reply.

"That will be three fifty plus tax," the saleslady commented, then paused and continued, "perhaps you would be interested in a special this manufacturer is offering for this week only. For eight dollars you get the lipstick plus a bottle of cologne, a bottle of powder base and a stick deodorant. Separately they would total ten dollars; so you save two dollars by taking the package."

The customer hesitated, then looked at the items and exclaimed, "I believe I'll take them. It seems to be a good value."

She could have added that she had been sold a package through the application of the give her something extra technique. Chances are good, however, that she will never use the cologne or powder base. Maybe they'll make nice little presents for Aunt Emma and Cousin Susan, come Christmas.

MONEY—THE NAME OF THE GAME

There may be other motives that prompt a buyer to want to buy from you, but the single most compelling reason is to make a profit for himself. Money always has been and always will be the name of the game in any seller-buyer relationship. Acquisition of money through profitable sales is the reason for his being a buyer. The buyer wants what he believes is best for himself. Everything else is automatically relegated to a secondary position. He therefore has to sell himself on your product's profitability before he will invest his money in it. You may sway him through persuasion and pressure, but in the last analysis, he is the one who makes the final decision as to whether he will or will not buy.

Concentrate On The Buyers's Interests

Selling, in truth, is a conflict of interest between the salesperson and the buyer:

1. Your interest as a salesperson is to make money for *yourself* by consummating the sale.
2. The buyer buys only because he is convinced that he can make money for *himself* on your product.

If you permit your own interests to become the predominating force behind your presentation, you will have trouble talking your way to successful sales. Too often there is a tendency for you to think too much in terms of yourself instead of what is best for the buyer. Concentrate on his viewpoint instead of your own, and you both win. Think in terms of what is best for his interests instead of your own, and you will both make money.

Use Paper And Pencil Selling To Increase Sales

The basic reason for your customer being in business is to create a profit from his operation. If he becomes convinced that your products are not profitable for him, you have your work cut out for you. One way to change his mind is to show him that he is wrong. In order to do this, you have to know all about his business. That's where *paper and pencil selling* can help you.

Do you know the difference between markup on cost and markup on selling price, and which of the two is normally used in most businesses? If you do, by calculating actual markup figures on paper, you can show your buyer how profitable your products can be for him. If you don't know how to figure markups, you better start doing some homework.

You can use pencil and paper selling to advantage in other aspects of his business. Show him on paper how he can reduce his inventory and create faster turnover by putting in a better stock control system. Put down figures that will prove to him that by reducing selling prices on dead inventory items, he can create a flow of money that will enable him to sweeten his stock and thereby increase his profitability.

There is much more to selling than presenting something to a buyer and trying to convince him that he should buy it from you. You also have to be able to talk his language—markups, markdowns, excessive inventory, dead inventory, stock controls, turnover, etc.

Jacques Millard, liason sales representative between a large home furnishings manufacturer and a major distributor, became concerned over their return on capital invested. He made a thorough analysis and was able to pinpoint the problem in three areas of their operation. Using paper and pencil selling and going into all specifics, he demonstrated that by putting in a new system of stock control and rearranging their warehouse storage, they could increase the efficiency of their operation and dam up the many leaks that were draining their profits.

Jacques spent many hours with management setting up new stock and stock control systems and he completely changed the in-and-out flow of merchandise in their warehouse. As a result, inventory was reduced and efficiency of warehouse operation was greatly increased.

The distributor started to make money. In six months, the president of the company offered Jacques a job as sales manager. Jacques took the job and started at a salary of $35,000, which was 70% more than he was getting at the time from the manufacturer.

Know-how plus some realistic paper and pencil selling certainly did pay off for Jacques Millard!

Use paper and pencil selling whenever you can. It will get results for you because the buyer knows you are knowledgeable about his business, and therefore has confidence in what you tell him and show him. Let your pencil show him the way to make money on your products. Let your pencil help you talk your way to increased sales.

Use Merchandising Aids To Work For You

You have to use every means at your disposal to maintain a steady pattern of profitable sales. In addition to selling skills and techniques, there are merchandising aids that can help you sell your products to the buyer, and help move them from the buyer's floor. Selling doesn't stop when you finalize a sale and your merchandise is shipped to the customer. Unless your products move off the sales floor and into the hands of the consumer, you will experience difficulty in getting orders on follow-up calls. Repeat business is the life blood of any good selling program, and these visual merchandising aids will help to insure a steady flow.

1. *Segregated displays* featuring your products will focus the buyer's attention on them. Keeping your products together and identifying them will help the consumer reach a buying decision.
2. *Advertising color reprints and blowups.* If your company does magazine advertising, accumulate all of the reprints and blowups you can get your hands on. They are excellent

for consumer use; they demonstrate visually how your product can be used.

3. *Color brochures and pamphlets.* Be sure your customer always has a good supply of these give-a-way items on hand to draw the consumer's interest. I once had a lady walk into our office with a color book that was so old it featured a pattern that had been discontinued ten years previously. She wanted to know where she could buy it.

   Go into almost any home and you'll find a kitchen drawer full of pictures, brochures, clippings, and other things being kept for future reference—perhaps for that memorable day when "I am finally going to get my new washing machine."

4. *Sales Contests.* This is something extra that makes people want to sell your products. Put up a trip to Bermuda or Hawaii as first prize in any selling contest, and they'll knock themselves out to support you.

5. *Animated and Moving Displays.* Use anything that will catch the buyer's eye. A moving display is a sure way to attract attention and put the power of suggestion to work.

6. *Slide Film Viewers.* Let the customer see pictures which show how others have adapted your product to their own use. Colored slide films dramatize any picture and create an interest in the viewer.

I can't think of a field that has more challenges and opportunities than the selling profession. As a salesperson, I am sure you have had your ups and downs, and there have probably been days when you wished you had stayed in bed. For the most part, however, selling can be very exciting and adventurous—sometimes even glamorous. Sure there are disappointments and frustrations, just as there are in any of life's experiences. But only a true salesperson knows the pure joy derived from the realization that he is "coming through" to the buyer—the feeling that he is winning the battle. It is second only to the thrill of finalizing the sale and writing the order.

3

SELLING SKILLS THAT HELP YOU TALK YOUR WAY TO SALES

Among the many experienced salespersons I talked with during the preparation of this book, there was one who advised me, "You're wasting your time worrying about selling skills and techniques and the rest of that baloney. All you need to make it big is a hot line of merchandise. If you have that, you can just walk in, expose it to the buyers, and they'll take it away from you. Get yourself a better mouse trap than the other guys have and the orders will come rolling in."

Mine is a contrary opinion. Having a good line of products is certainly a big plus, but I submit that the buyer won't take anything away from you. You may have the best quality product in your business, backed by excellent advertising and merchandising programs, but you have to *sell* it if you expect to get results. The better mouse trap just won't sell itself! You have to convince the buyer that it is profitable for him before he will part with his money.

To do this you must employ all the selling skills and techniques that are available to you. It is when your product has a reputation for being tops in quality in your field that it becomes even more necessary to do a top selling job. You are a sitting duck on top of the heap and all of your competitors are shooting at *you*.

USE THE FORCE OF HUMOR TO TALK YOUR WAY TO SUCCESSFUL SELLING

A major wholesale grocery company had a salesman named Oscar Lucke. Oscar was a little on the short side, obviously ate too much, was getting quite thin on top and had a face literally covered with wrinkles—from laughing. But Oscar had a secret. He had one of the most priceless possessions any salesperson could wish for, and that was his ability to make people smile and be happy.

Oscar always had a story for every occasion, and he was a master in timing them. He was at his very best telling jokes on himself. This man could walk into a room full of people with long faces and inside of ten minutes he would have them all laughing. It was little wonder that the buyers in his territory were always happy to see him.

Oscar came into sales the hard way—through the warehouse. He was one of the best stock men the company ever had and while he was working in the warehouse, it was, indeed, a "happy ship." At the suggestion of a major customer (who had met Oscar several times and was impressed by his humor and his generally happy disposition), management gave Oscar an opportunity in selling by assigning him to one of the poorest volume territories they serviced, fully expecting him to soon return to the warehouse.

But Oscar and his sense of humor fooled them. Within eighteen months he increased dollar sales in his territory, 100%! He had increases every year thereafter for the next five years. Then he was brought in to become assistant to the sales manager to handle large multiple store accounts, and to act as "trouble shooter" when the other salespersons ran into problems.

Oscar stayed on that assignment until he retired. At the time, he was making $29,000 per year. Not bad for someone who got his start in a warehouse! He had good product and know-how. However, it was Oscar's humor that put him where he was. He often said, "They won't stay mad long if you get them to smile." And Oscar certainly kept them smiling.

We can't all be like Oscar, but we can learn from him and perhaps in some small measure share his secret with him.

The Importance of Learning To Like People

Forget about yourself and your problems and start to concentrate on what makes the other guy tick. The best way to find yourself is to lose yourself in others and their problems. I can't think of any other profession than selling in which the need to like people is so necessary. A dentist doesn't have to like the patient whose teeth he is working on; the doctor may detest the patient he is treating; the lawyer might have an aversion to his client. And yet, all can be successful.

Selling is different. I can't conceive of any salesperson doing an effective job who doesn't truly like people. In fact, I have never known a top salesperson who didn't like people. That is not to say, however, that you never run across people whose "guts you hate." Sometimes there is a kind of chemical mix-up, or you are not on the same wave length, but I have found one thing to be true—people whom you dislike usually dislike you also.

As a salesperson, you can't afford to dislike any of your buyers or have any of them dislike you. Either way, *you* are the loser. Do everything you can to change your own attitude toward them. When you do this, you will accomplish two things: (1) you will win them over to liking you; and (2) you will get more business.

There's Nothing Like A Good Joke To Open The Door

A good story is one of the surest ways to break the ice with your customer. I am not referring to smut or filth, but cute stories that have a point, even though they may be just a little risqué. One precautionary **rule**: Never make your customer the butt of your joke. That's one sure way to get his nose bent. Conversely, you can make him like you by making *yourself* the goat of your story.

Jack Benny was an expert in using this skill. We all remember how he deliberately tried to give the radio and TV audiences an impression that he was a tightwad when in fact he was reported to be a very generous individual. He succeeded as a comedian by making himself the laughing stock of his own jokes. Look at all the famous comedians throughout the years and you will find that most of them used this technique.

How often we hear someone say, "I hear so many stories—I wish I could remember them." You can. Just get yourself a little notebook and start today to make reminder notes on jokes and stories you hear. As you fill its pages you will soon discover that you will have a joke or story to suit almost every occasion. Good story tellers are always welcome.

Harry Pinter was a "job-hopper." He was a good salesman, and everyone liked him because of his great sense of humor, but he never seemed to stay on the same job more than two years. Five jobs in ten years isn't a very good track record.

One day when he was chairman of his service club, the speaker didn't show up. Harry, feeling responsible, took the podium for a half hour and kept the audience in stitches with his stories, some about his own experiences. One of the visitors was Jack Brown, the head of a large insurance agency. He asked Harry afterwards if he would give the same talk two weeks later at his own service club.

Harry complied and following that meeting Brown asked to see him in his office. He told Harry, "You're a natural for insurance and I could use you. I'm the kind of person who always comes to the point. Are you happy with your present job and how much money are you making?"

Harry replied, "I guess my commissions will be around $18,000 this year. I'll be honest, though—I'm not too happy selling white goods."

Brown told him that he could train Harry in insurance and with his obvious talents and love of people (as demonstrated by his wonderful sense of humor), he would be making double that amount in four years. Brown proved to be right.

Harry joined him and in four years he was making $40,000. Had it not been for the impression he made on Brown that day at his club meeting, Harry might have gone on for years switching jobs and getting nowhere—just stumbling his way through life.

Harry's fame as a luncheon speaker spread, and soon he was booked up for weeks ahead. Much of his success in insurance was due to the people he met while speaking. Everything snowballed for Harry in the right direction. It all started because of his sense of humor, which, combined with his know-how led him to achieve success in insurance.

Never Upstage Your Buyer

If your customer tells you a corny joke that you have already heard ten times, act like it is the first time you ever heard it. Make him think that he has told a real knee slapper. If you want to make brownie points with your buyer, let him enjoy your jokes, but under no circumstances should you ever use those fatal words, "I've heard that one before," when he starts to tell one of his own. Make your buyer think he's the greatest story teller this side of the north pole.

Use Good Timing In Telling Your Jokes And Stories

The best story tellers use their talenst to fit given situations. There is magic in the words, "that reminds me of a story." The prophet tells us, "to every thing there is a season, and a time to every purpose ." There is a time to make jokes and a time to be serious. Recognizing the proper time is a skill in itself.

Properly used, a joke or good story can be of great help to you in talking your way to a sale; but improperly used, it can tear you apart.

Probably the worst kind of oaf is the guy who always tries to be funny when actually, he isn't. You have seen him many times—the insipid exhibitionist who tries to impress his buyers and is nothing but a bore. When you cut him down to size, you'll usually discover that his antics are a cover-up for an inferiority complex. This breed of arm-grabbing, back-slapping salesperson went out with button shoes, spats and the cigar store Indian.

USE THE POWER OF SIMPLICITY FOR EFFECTIVE SELLING

Take a lesson from the golf professionals on tour. They all swing easily, in simple, disciplined, and smooth patterns—and they knock the ball a mile. Too often salespersons press themselves and defeat their own objectives by making things too complicated. They either don't understand, or they forget, the power of simplicity.

While sitting in the club car of a train as it sped through the Pennsylvania countryside, the gentleman next to me told about Frank Sissonne, president of a mid-western bank.

Frank's college education was interrupted with the advent of World War II. Badly wounded when a kamikaze pilot struck his ship, he spent months in the hospital. He came out patched up, but undaunted. He went to work as a floor salesman for a large farm equipment company which had an active branch in his home town. Working on straight salary, Frank realized that he wouldn't get far, so he asked if he could start calling on farmers on a commission basis. Within a year he increased his income 100%—his commissions almost matched his salary. He subsequently went to work for his bank as a teller, at less money than he had been making selling. He had always wanted to get into banking, and being a salesman by nature within two years he was put in charge of loans, and within two more years he became loan and trust officer. His income was 250% greater than when he started with the bank. He subsequently went on to become president.

My seating companion explained, "Frank is a sharp individual, but the one single quality that makes for his success is his simplicity in everything he does. He always uses one and two syllable words and comes right to the point. When he opens his mouth, you don't have to guess what he is talking about. The farmers can understand him and as a result they identify with him. I never knew a man who could say so much in so few words. But that's Frank Sissonne—simplicity personified. No wonder he is the president of that bank today!"

Sam Goldwyn was one of the biggest producers in Hollywood. He was also a man who believed in the simple approach. The story is told that one day he was holding a meeting with the top people who would be involved in the production of a proposed outdoor spectacular film. The director thought the picture should be made in Idaho. Another had a spot picked out in Africa which he considered just right as a setting for the film. Others at the meeting suggested different areas—all involving costly travel and location expenses.

Throughout this discussion, Goldwyn sat in silence, listening. He finally rose and settled the whole matter with a simple observation: "A rock is a rock; a tree is a tree—we'll shoot it in Griffith Park." No muss; no fuss. Just an uncomplicated statement of fact that everyone in that room understood.

The P.S. to this story is that the picture was actually shot in Griffith Park within ten miles from the studio. Sam Goldwyn was not only one of the most successful producers in the motion picture industry, but he was also a fine salesman. He used the power of simplicity to make his point, and thereby saved his company hundreds of thousands of dollars in travel and location expenses.

No book on salesmanship would be complete without some mention of the Master Salesman of all time. That there was, in fact, a man named Jesus Christ is a proven historical fact. I have no intention of getting into any hassles on the subject of theology, but I respectfully submit that Jesus has had more of an impact on the lives of the people of this world than any other man who ever lived. He has been called the Divine Healer and the Great Teacher. In the context of this book, I call Him the Master Salesman—the Super Salesman of all time. Just think—with an organization of twelve men, (most of whom were illiterate and uneducated), he took an idea—a concept of a new way of life—and under seemingly impossible conditions sold it to the people of His time and made the sale stick for 2000 years!

One can't read His words without having an awareness of His magnificent simplicity. Jesus used parables because He knew He could put His message across by drawing simple word pictures that the people of His day could understand.

I have found that complexity, affectation, intricacy and the like are usually cover-ups for lack of product knowledge and know-how. Don't ever get the notion that by using fancy words and otherwise muddying the waters you will be able to deceive your buyer. If you think you can achieve your objective through confusion, forget it. It won't work. Fast talking never has been and never will be a substitute for down-to-earth simplicity.

WHEN YOU ARE TALKING, SAY IT WITH SINCERITY

If you expect to be a success in the selling business, you have to not only believe in yourself and your own capabilities, but also in the product you are selling. Otherwise you will have difficulty in being sincere with your buyer.

Many companies have "think tanks" at their home offices whose purpose is to develop new merchandising ideas and products. Every now and then they come up with things that just don't seem to ring a bell with their sales representatives. When that happens, their salespersons can't go out and do an effective selling job because they don't believe in what they are selling. When a salesperson doesn't believe in something, he is reluctant to try to foist it off on his customers.

Clyde Birch, representative of a large manufacturer of household sundries once told another salesman, "we had a promotion on a new kind of self-polishing wax. I took a sample home and my wife tried it on our kitchen floor. It looked beautiful when first applied, but every time water hit it, white spots showed up on the floor. It just wasn't worth a damn! My people really slipped up on that one. Now I was expected to sell that wax, so I was faced with a decision. I either go ahead and sell it and say nothing about my kitchen floor, or come clean with my buyers and tell them not to buy it because we already have better wax products in our line.

"I chose the latter course. Apparently I wasn't the only one in our outfit who felt as I did, because not long thereafter that wax was suddenly withdrawn from the market. Being honest and sincere with my customers paid off for me because when we came out with an excellent new product later on, I sold the pants off it. The repeat business was unbelievable. That first year, on that wax alone, my commission was $2,000.00." Why? Simply because his customers believed what he told them.

I have been on both sides of the fence, in selling and district office sales management, and I feel qualified from practical experience to state: *there is absolutely no way that a salesperson can be persuaded to sell something he doesn't believe in.*

The story is told about a manufacturer of dog food. They were having their annual sales meeting for which all of their sales representatives had been brought in. Business hadn't been good and the charts looked bad. The sales manager stood on the podium, held a can of their dog food in his hand and asked, "Who has the best selling organization in the dog food business?" The audience gave a resounding, "*We have*!" He then waved the can in his hand and continued, "Who has the best looking can and the best advertising program in this industry?" Again the answer was a loud, "*We have*." After a long pause he demanded, "Then why in the hell don't we sell more dog food?"

There was a deadly silence, broken by a small voice from the rear of the room saying, "The dogs don't like it!"

All salespersons worth their salt are like those dogs. If you don't like it yourself and if you have no confidence in it, then how in the world can you ask your customers to buy it? You can't pull the wool over your buyer's eyes. If he gets the feeling that you are "putting him on," you're finished.

Being uncertain or vague are two marks of insincerity. If you are not always frank and honest with your buyer, you'll get yourself caught in a resistance quicksand from which you won't be able to extricate yourself. If he gets wise to you, he won't believe anything you tell him. When that happens, you might as well scoop up your marbles and leave.

USE THE SOFT SELL INSTEAD OF THE HARD SELL TO BE EFFECTIVE

One of the best salesmen I ever knew was a man who represented a steel products company. Everyone admired Duke for his finesse and skill. Nothing seemed to upset him—he always ran cool. He was an expert in setting up a game plan for each call and he always came to the point without any double talk or needless waste of time. Duke was not known as a pressure salesman—he appeared to always be in low gear. He used the soft sell technique, but he applied intense pressure on his buyers without their being aware of it.

Buyers were always happy to see Duke—they felt comfortable with him. None of that high pressure stuff, making them feel that they had to buy. His buyers didn't know it, but Duke was actually a high powered salesman. His subtlety verged on being almost insidious. He had a magical soft sell touch that hid the hammer he carried in his hand. He gave the buyers such a snow job they were completely unaware of the fact that he was putting the blocks to them. Very seldom would he walk away without an order.

Duke is no longer covering a territory—he is now sales manager for the company. I have no way of knowing what his salary is, but I would judge from his life style that his income is somewhere around $60,000 annually. He made it because he was a soft sell salesman. He is now a soft sell manager, and as a result he is getting excellent production from his salespersons.

A lesson to be learned from Duke is; if you feel that pressure is indicated to put across a sale with a particular buyer, don't be obvious about it! Most buyers are intuitive through experience, and they will back away once they get the feeling that you are trying to put the screws to them. You can blow your sale if you get over anxious and start to *hard sell* and pressure your buyer.

We have all had the experience of walking into an automobile showroom to buy a car, and running across two types of salespersons. First, there is the one who stays right on your tail, talking constantly, giving you no time to think for yourself, trying to convince you that you should and must buy a car on the spot. He lets you drive a demonstrator, but he climbs in the seat beside you. This is the hard sell salesperson. Then, there is the soft sell person who stands by, lets you look around, and carefully and courteously answers your questions. He suggests you take a ride in a demonstrator, but doesn't go with you.

The second salesperson is just as anxious to sell you a car as the first one, but he doesn't wear a big buy sign with flashing red lights on his lapel. Be honest with yourself—which of these two would you rather do business with?

Harry Allens was a salesman for an automobile agency which handled one of the major medium and low priced cars. He was a typical soft sell salesman and he was successful. One day the owner called Harry in his office and said, "Harry, our fleet sales stink! We used to be big, but now we are peanuts. Somehow we've let it all slip away from us. I want you to take over. You can keep your present customers and I'll pay you a bonus above commission on fleet sales until you get things moving for us."

First Harry got the names of companies who had once bought from them. He then went over his own customers and learned from them the names of purchasing agents in companies they worked for. Harry then started making calls for appointments. In each instance on his first call, he said he was there just to get acquainted and made no effort to sell anything: he just wanted them to give him a chance on any future business. It was all low key—typically soft sell.

At the start, Harry was discouraged, but he hung in there. He drew a blank the first two months and then got a couple of small orders. It was when he got an order for thirty-four cars that he realized the possibilities in this end of the business. He doubled his efforts, and as a result of his commissions on fleet sales he increased his income $4,500 that first year. Even after the owner took off the special bonus incentive, Harry subsequently maintained a steady increase in fleet sales.

The purchasing agents liked Harry Allens because he didn't try to pressure them. One young salesman, who was somewhat of a table pounder, once asked Harry, "How do you do it, Harry?" Harry replied, "I carry soft pellets in my gun instead of bullets. I want to anesthesize my customers—not kill them."

In some lines of business, sales managers advocate the use of the double-up technique to produce sales. I don't agree that the technique of "two-timing" a buyer is generally effective, and therefore submit another contrary opinion. Whenever I saw two salesmen coming into my office to try to sell me something, I immediately put myself on guard and turned off my "buy button." Usually one gave the pitch and the other was the hard sell "closer." It may work with some, but in my judgment a salesperson is much better off to go it alone. If you need a closer to button up your sale for you, then there is something wrong with your own capabilities. It certainly doesn't constitute a vote of confidence in you by your management; or perhaps *they* should take a refresher course in good salesmanship.

A good salesperson must use the power of persuasion to be a success in his business. However, some fail to realize that there is such a thing as over-persuasion. It is a sad commentary that some salespersons seem to feel that table thumping and other outward indications of high pressure tactics are necessary for successful selling. Actually the opposite is true. It is important to be deliberate and forthright in your presentation, but that doesn't mean that you should beat the buyer in the head for the order.

Rule: Carry a big stick, but always keep it under wraps. You may not be a hard sell salesperson, but you must exercise care to make certain that your buyer doesn't think otherwise. There are two precautionary measures you can take to avoid wrong impressions:

1. *Never hover over your buyer.* This is particularly important if you happen to be a tall individual and your buyer is small. Always try to maneuver your buyer into a position where you are on an eye to eye level with him. If possible, go a step further and place yourself at a lower level. If he is seated, and you are standing, don't ever place your hands on his desk and lean toward him. Always ask, "May I sit down, please?" . . . if he doesn't offer you a seat. Do everything you can to avoid an impression that you are trying to overwhelm him.

2. *Never touch your buyer*. Don't grab him by the arm or poke your finger in his chest. Some salespersons are guilty of doing these things without thinking. Most buyers dislike it. To them, it is an outward display of high pressure selling. Use your hands to *show* the buyer, not to *touch* him.

Perhaps at this point you may think that I am cutting it just a little too thin, but I cannot overemphasize how small, seemingly unimportant things can have a bearing on the outcome of your sale. Your buyer is alert to everything you do and everything you say. Always bear in mind that if you come in on him like a lion, chances are good that you'll go out like a lamb.

USE THE FORCE OF ENTHUSIASM TO PUT PUNCH IN YOUR PRESENTATION

Enthusiasm is a propellant that often can have a profound effect on the success of your sales presentation. It is frequently one of the most misunderstood skills that a salesperson has at his disposal. This is probably due to the fact that enthusiasm is one of the intangibles of good salesmanship. Because it is something that comes from one's mind, it is very difficult to define.

Enthusiasm is definitely *not* rushing into your buyer's office, rubbing your hands together, and exclaiming, "Boy, oh boy—do I have something hot to show you!" If you think that approach will turn your buyer on, you are mistaken, because it is a sure way to turn his buying faucet off.

You don't have to *show* your buyer how enthusiastic you are—you have to make him *feel* it. When you say what you mean and mean what you say, you don't need trumpets and drums to tell your buyer about your enthusiasm. It all goes back to good product knowledge and know-how, without which genuine enthusiasm is impossible.

Sometimes an outward display of enthusiasm is a cover-up for basic inadequacies that the salesperson may have. Effervescence is nothing more than gas—it has no true substance. Don't be guilty of the kind of enthusiasm you see among football players just prior to the kick-off—jumping up and down as though they are on pogo sticks. This show of enthusiasm quickly disappears after the first play of the game when they run into the silent, hard hitting opposition.

If you are self-confident you can't help being enthusiastic about your work. If you don't have the "killer instinct," you'll always be running along in low gear. Lest you misunderstand what I mean by killer instinct, I define it as a strong desire to win, to make the sale. Some of the most mild-mannered salespersons I have known had it. As a matter of fact, I can't recall ever meeting a top salesperson who didn't possess this quality. Once you know you can make it you will automatically strive to improve your performance. The desire to win increases with each success. When you win the bronze medal, you work for the silver medal and then keep on going until they finally hang the gold medal around your neck.

I was told about Adam Lundquist, a representative of a small tire manufacturer, who had almost a phenomenal success in his field. He had been moved several times from one territory to another, and each time he would increase sales. He turned down all offers of management because he detested paper work. He wanted to sell, sell, sell!

When asked what the key to his success was, Lundy replied, "We may not be the biggest in the tire business, but I'll tell you something—we put out the best damned tire for the money! I may not be the best salesman in the world either, but I'll bump heads with any tire salesman any day in the week." It's little wonder that Lundy was a success. That kind of confidence and enthusiasm was bound to rub off on his customers. He was different from the run of the mill salesperson. He *expected* to sell his tires—so he did!

Major competitors were constantly after Lundy to hire him. They knew he was a good salesman because he was cutting into their business. One of them approached him one day with an offer to pay a higher percentage of commission than he was making. Lundy took it. He reasoned that if he could knock down $18,000 a year with the line he was handling, he should do much better with a known brand.

Lundy was right. He was prepared for a reduction in income for the first year, but surprised himself when he bettered it slightly. From then on it was an upward climb. Combining his know-how with the enthusiasm he generated for his new line of tires, within three years he was making better than $30,000 a year.

HOW TO STRENGTHEN YOUR PRESENTATION BY SAYING IT QUICKLY

A guest speaker at a Rotary Club luncheon once made a thought-provoking statement. He said, "The attention span of a three-year-old child is approximately one minute, while that of most adults is in the area of ten minutes." At first I found that hard to believe, but the more I thought about it and watched others, the more I realized that he wasn't too far from the truth.

Unless you have the undivided attention of your buyer, you will have a tough time getting him to buy your package. Instead of dilly-dallying and beating around the bush, make your point quickly if you expect to make it stick. Once he loses his concentration and his mind begins to wander to other things, you have lost him.

Ten minutes. That's all the time you have. Make the most of it.

WHY HUMILITY IS AN EFFECTIVE SELLING SKILL

One word that more than any other best characterized Abraham Lincoln was his humility. President during one of the most trying periods of our nation, he was often forced to take stands that were unpopular with many in his government. As a result of his steadfastness and humility, he was respected by friends and foes alike. His humility was the glue that helped to hold the country together, saving it from total disintegration.

Humility is in no way a cover-up for any lack of confidence. On the contrary, the humble person is usually a strong, knowledgeable individual. It is the conceited, arrogant salesperson who usually lacks self-confidence. Most buyers will tell you that there is nothing worse than a salesperson who is a braggart. They are constantly bragging about how much money they are making and how successful they are. They are like men who brag about their conquests with women, when in truth they're usually all talk and little production.

Nobody likes a smart-aleck, least of all your buyers. It isn't necessary to show your confidence and flaunt it before him. That is one sure way to irritate him and cool him off. When you let him know that you have all of the answers, he has only one answer—to get rid of you as quickly as possible.

Have you ever known a name-dropper? He's the kind of salesperson who tries to impress the buyer with the people he knows. So your sister-in-law's ex-husband was once a State Senator! Who cares? Usually, people who lack humility make fools of themselves. A salesperson can't afford to put himself in that light with his buyers.

Humility can, indeed, be a powerful selling skill. A humble salesperson doesn't hesitate to admit to the buyer that he doesn't have an answer to a given problem or situation. He is quick to use seven important words—*I don't know,—I'll check it out.* If your buyer asks you a question and you're not sure of the answer, don't guess! You cannot afford to take chances and make any mistakes with his money. Admit that you don't know, but that you will find out. He will respect you for your humility and also for your wisdom.

The owner of a large lumber mill who also operated a chain of retail outlets once told me, "Not long ago one of my key men came to me and announced that he was retiring early on the advice of his doctor. I wasn't prepared for this turn of events but knew that I had to find someone to replace him. Doing this was more difficult than I at first anticipated. I had to decide which of my retail store managers I would 'kick upstairs'. The choice finally boiled down to three men, all good salesmen and also darned good store managers. After giving it a lot of thought, I finally chose Walter, because—well, he seemed to be more of a solid citizen than the others. I guess it was his humility that made the difference. The way things worked out, I made the right decision." Walter moved from a job paying him $25,000 annually to one where his base pay was $45,000 annually. His humility made the difference!

What are the marks of a salesperson who has humility?

1. He has a respect for the opinions of others.
2. He has the ability to say "thank you" and really mean it.
3. He is a peacemaker.
4. He has confidence but is not overly aggressive.
5. He always speaks with sincerity.
6. He has a consciousness of his own shortcomings.
7. He is usually quiet and reserved.
8. He usually says little—is a good listener.
9. He avoids extremes—does things in moderation.
10. He does not brag or boast.

Check yourself off against these qualities of humility. How do you stand? Would you, like Walter, be selected for promotion because of your humility? Since humility is an effective skill, it will pay you to consider applying these marks to your own selling arsenal.

WHEN YOU ARE TALKING—SAY IT CHEERFULLY

So often we have all heard salespersons say, "I sure hate this rat race. I wish I could get into something else," or "There must be an easier way to make a living," or "I hate this traveling, living in motels half my life," or "My boss is a first class s.o.b. He has been away from selling so long, he has forgotten our problems." They all have one thing in common. These people don't enjoy their work. Unfortunately for them, their buyers quickly discover their discontent and react unfavorably toward them.

We all get down in the dumps at times, but when you begin to feel sorry for yourself and decide that you don't like what you're doing, consider the alternatives before you act in haste. I suggest that you take a blank sheet of paper, draw a line down the center, and then head the two sides with the captions, *What I like about my job,* and *What I don't like about my job.* It has been the experience of many who have tried this that their job isn't so bad after all! Remember one thing—winning isn't always easy!

Walt Disney was one of the top salespersons of modern times. He knew that while people mature with age, they never lose the little child in them. He proved this through the brilliance of his animated cartoons, so that today his little characters are household pets for all. One beautiful thing about his cartoons was the fact that they usually carried a message for us all. I often think of those seven dwarfs who "whistled while they worked." How wonderful it would be if we all were like those dwarfs and could whistle while *we* work!

You can do this. Being cheerful is something over which you have control, because it is a state of mind. Being cheerful in your work not only makes you happy but rubs off on your buyer as well. You are creating a positive attitude that makes him receptive to you.

Al Harkins, an account executive for a large stock and bond house, is outwardly one of the most cheerful persons one could hope to meet. He never complains about anything and always greets his clients with a big smile. And yet, if they but knew what he has gone through in the course of the past few years, they would wonder how he does it. In less than four years he lost his mother and father, was divorced by his wife, and had one son disappear without any trace of his whereabouts. Instead of blaming the world and everyone in it for his troubles, he takes the opposite approach toward life and tries to see the good instead of the bad. As a result, despite the tragedies that beset him he has become a very successful salesman. During this period when most men would have folded their tents, Al increased the number of his clients 28% and at the same time increased his income 34%. People like to do business with Al because he is always so pleasant. A man like that is made of pretty tough stuff.

Rule: You can't smile and be mad at the same time—so keep your buyer smiling.

4

HOW TO GET OTHERS TO HELP YOU TALK YOUR WAY TO SUCCESSFUL SALES

Even experienced salespersons often become so involved with the buyer that they completely overlook other people who can be influential in helping them talk their way to sales. You need all the assistance you can get and you simply cannot afford to overlook anyone. The people around the buyer as well as others who have no relationship with him can frequently provide for you the key you need to open the door to a sale. Always remember that the most beautiful sound in the world to any person is the sound of his own name. Regardless of who we are, or how menial or relatively unimportant our role in life may be, we all have one thing in common. We crave the respect of others and thrive on recognition.

There are five areas where you can look for help: 1) the people around the buyer; 2) your associates in your company; 3) salespersons handling non-related products; 4) your other customers; and 5) others whom you contact each day.

HOW TO GET HELP FROM THE PEOPLE AROUND THE BUYER

The people around the buyer are almost as important to you as the buyer himself. He often relies on them for advice, and what they tell him concerning your products can depend a great deal on how you have treated them. I learned from hard experience that they can either make you or annihilate you.

Many of the lessons that stuck closest to my ribs came early in my selling days, when I was young and impressionable. I was at one time assigned to a new territory, and my predecessor spent a week with me calling on some of the accounts. Buck was an amazing salesman. I remember well our first call. Before he went into the buyer's office, he sought out every other employee in the store and introduced me to them. He called them all by their names, and everybody in the place knew him by name. They seemed genuinely glad to see him—the janitor who swept the floor, the salesmen, the craftsmen in the back room, the girls in the office. When it came time to go to the buyer's office and Buck introduced me, the buyer said, "Sorry boys, but I don't have any time for you today. I have a little tax problem I'm working on, so if you'll excuse me . . . " To which Buck quickly replied, "That's OK, Mr. Sanderson. Phil here will catch you on his next trip."

When we got outside, I said, "Well, we sure struck out there in a hurry."

I'll never forget Buck's reply. "No, we didn't Phil. We did a good job of selling you to all of those people in the store. You keep them in your camp and the orders will come for you. They can do you a lot of good or they can really hurt you—it's strictly up to you."

I learned the wisdom of Buck's remark when I discovered that in three years on the territory I was taking over, he had increased dollar volume 32%. I knew I had my work cut out for me.

Not long ago I asked one of our men, "When was the last time you took a craftsman out to lunch?" When he was hesitant in answering I continued, "Did you ever stop to think how much good a craftsman can do for you, and conversely, how much harm?" I always made certain that the men who installed our products were happy. I sought them out and listened to them to make sure that they were on my team. These men can raise havoc by making comments to the buyer, putting doubts in his mind concerning your product. Be sure they take their complaints to *you* instead of the buyer.

Everyone around the buyer is important to you. In the course of a career in selling, one runs across strange situations and unusual people. One so-called salesman had a chauffeur who not only drove for him but also accompanied him on every call, walking behind, carrying his samples and selling case. I couldn't believe my eyes the first time I saw him. He didn't look right or left, and spoke to no one. After he had finished with the buyer, he strutted out, again saying nothing to others in the store, his lackey trailing behind him. He handled a good line, was able to talk his way to sales with the buyers, but the inevitable happened. The floor salespersons, the craftsmen, and everyone else went out of their way to knock his products with the result that they didn't move off the floor. They resented this stuffed-shirt salesman, who didn't even *look* at anyone else in the store, so they killed his business by putting their kiss of death on his products. He wasn't long on the territory—this is truly an "unsuccess story."

For several years, one of the largest flooring contractors in the territory handled a competitive line of tile. We knew that he was doing a big volume of business in the tract housing field, but nothing that our men did could persuade him to switch to our line. One of our competitors seemed to have him "locked in." We finally made it, but while the tune of "Happy Days Are Here Again" reverberated from the walls of our offices, we were sobered by our knowledge that one man was largely responsible, Jimmy Calhoun, an estimator-salesman who worked for the customer. Because our own men and the wholesaler's men had befriended him with a little golf and a dinner now and then, he developed a warm feeling toward us and our products. When the opportune time came, Jimmy was able to convince the buyer that our product would do a better job for him. This man talked our way to one of the biggest sales we ever made. We and our wholesaler benefitted from dollar volume of $150,000 from that one customer during a twelve month period.

Did it pay us to be friendly with the people around the buyer? You better believe it!

Recently I was sitting in a crowded reception room waiting to see my doctor, when I observed a pharmaceutical salesman at work. The receptionist called him by his first name and I noticed that the nurses began to show up behind the glass partitioned enclosure, all giving him a friendly greeting. I watched as he took samples from his case and although I couldn't hear the conversation, I knew he was talking about his products. One of the nurses then motioned to him and he followed her down a corridor. He came out ten minutes later, again going to the receptionist to say a few words before he departed. After I saw the doctor, I returned to the waiting room and walked over to the receptionist.

I said, "Jeannie, would you answer a question for me?"

"I'll be glad to," was her reply.

"Did that salesman who was in here with that case full of samples get to see the doctor?" I asked.

"Oh yes. We always let him in. He is so nice to everyone. He sometimes even brings in flowers for us. All of the girls are crazy about him. He's so friendly!"

I can well imagine that getting to see and talk business with a busy doctor is a rough assignment for any salesperson, but this man made it because he won the admiration of the people around him. That reception desk—in fact any reception desk in any business—can be a real iron curtain for you. The only way to break it is to make friends with those who control it. The salesman I saw knew what he was doing. He used a "three F" skill to good advantage to get through the barrier to see the doctor—flattery, friendliness, and flowers. Then I got curious, perhaps even to the point of being nosy. I asked Jeannie if the drug salesman ever told her how well he was doing financially on the territory. The only answer I got on my "fishing expedition" was, "All I know is he started out four years ago driving a Datsun just like the fellow who called on us before him. Now he is driving an El Dorado." That in itself told me the story. He was an expert in getting the people around the buyer to work for him, and made it pay off for himself.

A sales representative for a distributor handling refrigerators, stoves, and other appliances, once told me, "When I am showing a new line, the buyer will often call in his floor salespersons to ask them what they think of it. Whether they say, 'Great—it's what we need. It looks like a hot item,' or 'It's too much like some of the things we already have. I don't think we need it,' depends in a large measure on how much time I have spent with them and how effective I have been in winning them over to my side. In many ways these people are more important than the buyer himself."

Salespersons who are selling to the consumer can knock your products out with little comments such as, "I know it's pretty, but it doesn't have the quality of this other line," or "This is just as good, but costs you less, because this company doesn't spend a lot of money on advertising like the other one does, so they can sell cheaper." Conversely, they can help you by telling the consumer, "I recommend this because its the very best value."

One interesting case example of how a salesperson talked his way to more sales was told to me by one of our other district managers. Ed Jackson, one of his salesmen, had been calling on a large specialty shop in the metropolitan area for almost a year. He was getting some business from this customer but only a relatively small percentage. When orders started to come in and volume built up, the manager asked him what he was doing to turn things around with this account.

Jackson told him, "I went bowling one night and in the alley next to me were several of the salesmen from this store. They were in a league and bowled every Thursday night, but they weren't doing too well. I had a real good game myself that night and when one of them saw my scores he asked if I would be interested in joining their team. To make a long story short, I did, and I not only became the anchor man on their team, but naturally we all became friends. They started to push business my way and, well, the orders came rolling in—just like ten strikes. My business with the customer increased 300% in a year's time."

You can't all join bowling teams, but the important lesson is that there are many ways in which you can get to the people who surround the buyer, people who can have an important influence in helping you talk your way to increased sales.

I suggest that you make an honest evaluation of how you stack up with the people who are working for and with the buyer. Do you go out of your way to try to be nice to them? Are you sincerely interested in them? If you find that you are concentrating too much on the buyer in trying to talk your way to sales, take some time and effort to enroll these other people on your team just by being friendly with them.

When you start out on a program to make friends with these people, use the *rifle approach* instead of spraying your shots. Pick out one individual on each call and go to work on him. You will be amazed at the reaction. You will not only get help from him at times when you really need it, but you will find that talking your way to sales becomes more enjoyable as well as more profitable.

HOW TO GET HELP FROM PEOPLE IN YOUR OWN COMPANY

When you are talking your way to sales, always remember you are a part of a team effort. You are carrying the ball, to be sure, but you must rely on others to block for you and help you score. Not a day passes that you aren't in some way involved with others in your organization; an order clerk, the credit manager, a shop foreman, or a stenographer. How well do you get along with these people? Are you friendly with them or do you treat them like lackeys? Do you give them the recognition and respect that they so eagerly crave or do you just fluff them off as a necessary part of your work? How you answer these questions will tell how helpful they are to you when you need them. If you expect the support of others in your organization, it only follows that you must be willing to do things for them. Nothing can rip a salesperson apart more than having some stenographer or shipping clerk screw up on a detail that costs him a sale. However, when that does happen, it is more than likely that he brought it on himself.

Jess Wiley, one of my salesmen, came to me one day and complained that the girls in the office always put his letters at the bottom of the pile and showed a preference to the other salespersons. I had my secretary check into the matter and was quite surprised when she told me he was right. The stenographers admitted that Jess was put last because of his general attitude and the fact that his least wish became an emergency. Actually, the basic problem was that he felt that he was a cut above others in the company who had more menial positions than his and he showed it!

We had a nice little chat about the situation and when Jess finally realized how important the people around him were, he changed his ways and things got back on the track. He became cooperative and the stenographers were happy. He didn't bug them, and they turned out his work for him.

How often do you sit down with other salespersons in your own organization to discuss your mutual problems? You can learn much from the seasoned veterans. Get next to those who are successful. Pick their brains and find out what skills and techniques they use to talk their way to successful sales. Cross-fertilization of ideas among a group of salespersons can be extremely helpful not only to the organization but to each individual as well.

Selling skills and techniques aren't learned overnight. Acquiring them comes only from years of experience. Most managers encourage a close relationship among their salespersons who can help one another through an exchange of ideas and helpful tips.

You should make certain that you are also on the same wave length as your boss. It is definitely to his advantage to counsel you when you have problems, because his success or failure is largely dependent upon the effectiveness of his sales organization. He is therefore not only interested in your activities, but also wants to be helpful to you. Don't be afraid of him. He sometimes has to take a hard stand, but remember—he has many responsibilities. Encourage him to call on your key accounts with you. This gives him an opportunity to see the customer's own home court, but of greater significance, makes the customer feel important to have the big boss taking the time to call on him.

Let your manager sit alone in the office with the buyer and give the latter an opportunity to let off steam if he is dissatisfied with anything. Buyers will often let down their hair with the top brass in your office. This probably stems from the fact that they feel on equal grounds with him. Don't let that bother you as long as you are getting his business. Never resent your boss—some day you may be sitting at his desk. In the meantime, use his knowledge of skills and techniques to help you talk your way to successful sales.

Gain the confidence of your credit manager. Keep him posted on any unusual developments concerning your accounts. Help him and he'll help you when you might need him on a large job. Understand the three C's of credit—capital, character, and capacity. Try to get your credit manager to make calls with you on your key accounts. This not only enables him to keep himself updated on what is happening in your territory, but also gives your customer an opportunity to talk about credit matters in his own office. Credit can sometimes be a "sticky" subject and create hard feelings, so it behooves you to keep as close as possible to your credit manager.

Finally, make friends with the men in the shipping department. They can hurt you by delaying a rush shipment and doing other things that can get you in the middle between your company and your customer. Howard Heyton, one of our best wholesaler salesmen, once said to me, "I never walk through the front door of our plant. I always go through the rear so I can say 'hello' to the boys in the shipping and receiving departments. I'll tell you—its good business to josh with them. You never know when you'll need them."

It was more than coincidental that several weeks after Howard Heyton told me why he always walked through the back door to visit with the warehousemen, one of the latter saved him and his company from a costly error.

Howard turned in an order for 680 cartons of pattern 860—one of the colors of tile handled. Somehow, one of the people in the office made a mistake in writing up the shipping instructions and wrote down 860 cartons of pattern 680, an entirely different color. Shipment was to be made direct to the job for immediate installation. It so happened that Howard had asked the shipping clerk a week before to check if they had plenty of pattern 860 in stock because he had a big job coming up.

When the shipping instructions hit his desk, the shipping clerk was puzzled so he called the office to check and found that in transposing the order the numbers had inadvertently been reversed.

Can you image what would have happened if pattern 680 had actually been shipped and was installed on the job? Just because Howard always made it a point to walk through the back door, a costly mistake was avoided.

If you are neglecting or avoiding these people start today to enter the back door and make yourself known to them. Always bear in mind that whenever anyone in your shipping department fouls up, *you* are the one whom your customer blames. Conversely they can do things for you by giving you that "extra service" that sometimes can make the difference between getting or losing a sale.

HOW TO GET HELP FROM SALESPERSONS HANDLING NON-RELATED PRODUCTS

If you haven't made it a practice to get acquainted with other salespersons working in your territory, start in today. You will be surprised at the help they can give you. If you are a salesperson, you just can't afford to be a loner. Meet others in your profession, make friends with them, talk to them and exchange ideas. You will find that by so doing they can help you increase your own effectiveness in talking your way to sales.

A case in point involves Jim Turnbull, a mattress salesman with whom I had developed a friendly relationship. Many of my customers also bought from him. In addition to his line of box springs and mattresses which he sold to furniture stores and specialty shops, he also had a line of hospital furniture: metal beds, night stands and other equipment, as well as springs and mattresses. Jim telephoned me at home one evening and asked me to meet him the following night in the hotel of one of the cities where we often met. He told me he didn't want to explain over the phone but it would be worth my while to meet him. Knowing him as I did, I agreed to join him.

When I met him I asked, "What's up, Jim?"

He replied, "I'm working on a real 'sleeper' and I think I can get you in on the act. I have an appointment early in the morning with the owner of a new convalescent home. I have seen him before but he wants to finalize the order tomorrow. It's a nice chunk of business for me."

"That's nice, Jim, but where do *I* fit in?" I asked.

He replied, "We got to talking about floors and he asked for my recommendations. I told him I knew just the man who had all the answers—namely, you. He's hot to trot, so as soon as I am finished with my business, we'll sell him the floor. The same dealer who handles my stuff can put in the floor covering."

I won't go into all the details of this transaction, but as a result of Jim's interest and intercession on my behalf, I met the owner and was able to talk my way to a very successful sale. To be more accurate, I should say that Jim and I talked my way to the sale, because he was right there helping me.

It was a nice order in itself—$4,500. The frosting on the cake, however, came when the owner of the convalescent home requested that Royal Floors make the installation. They had previously purchased very little of our materials, favoring one of our competitors. However, as a result of a satisfactory and profitable relationship stemming from the convalescent home job, we started to get business from Royal. Our total business with Royal that year amounted to $15,000.

We maintained a good position with Royal in the years to come all because of a good relationship with Jim Turnbull, a mattress salesman! He had opened the door for us!

An interesting aside to this story is the fact that less than six months later I was able to return Jim's favor. I helped him salvage one of his important accounts who had threatened to throw out his line because of an error made by his credit department. Having a friendly relationship paid off for both of us.

If you are missing the opportunity to get acquainted with men such as Jim in your own work, you are not taking advantage of the help they can give you. Like many other experienced salespersons you may be letting yourself get bogged down in the quagmire of your own business to a point that you don't think of giving consideration to what others can do for you.

Another example of benefiting from a close relationship with a salesperson handling a non-related line is the case of a wholesale drug salesman who specialized in selling prescription bottles to druggists. Al said he had been trying for some time to crack a chain of drug stores who could give him a sizable volume of business, but all he got from the centralized buyer who handled all of the purchasing was a lot of conversation, but no orders.

Al was having dinner one evening with Cooper, another salesman who handled sundry lines and also called on drug stores. He told him about the problem he was having breaking into the account that had been bugging him. Cooper said, "I know Smith real well—buys a lot from me. Trouble with him is he is too darned lazy to want to make a change in anything. Tell me, how do your prices compare with others?" When Al told him his prices were competitive and in addition his company had some exclusive features in the caps for their prescription bottles, Cooper continued, "I'll talk to Smith next time I call on him and see what I can do for you."

Al then went on to say, "I don't get all of his business, but as a result of my friend's putting in a good word for me, I was able for the first time to get my foot in the door with this buyer. My commission on sales to this account amounted to $1,100.00 the first year—all pure gravy as far as I was concerned. I never could have made it without his help. That taught me a lesson I'll not soon forget. I now talk to everyone. Believe me, you never know when somebody will give you the push you so badly need to get the right entree with a buyer."

How well do you know the other salespersons who are working in your territory? Do you make it a point to sit down with them now and then over a lunch table to compare notes, or do you go about your own business and ignore others? I don't care who he is—you can always learn something from someone else. It all boils down to that very simple and human formula of you scratch my back, and I'll scratch yours. How well are *you* scratching?

LET YOUR OTHER CUSTOMERS HELP YOU TALK YOUR WAY TO SALES

Satisfied customers can be a gold mine of new and additional business if you will enlist their help. Doctors and lawyers build their business on referrals made by their contented patients and clients. Through the use of skills and expertise available to them, one satisfied "customer" tells another. The same can be true in the selling profession, both at the wholesale and retail levels.

A professor in salesmanship at a large university made it a practice to seek out and invite successful businessmen to speak before his class. One who was invited was the owner of a commercial maintenance company. Mr. Thorenson had started his business with a ladder, a bucket, a sponge, a squeegee, and a lot of ambition.

He told the students, "I washed windows for a big company that went broke not long after I went to work for them. Times were tough and I was out of a job for quite a spell. I had to eat, so I took my bucket and squeegee and started ringing doorbells. I guess I was lucky because I got some business right away. Then it dawned on me that instead of continuing to knock on doors for new business, I would let my customers help me branch out. I thought up my *perform and pursue system* which to this day is the motto of my company. I never left a job without first going over my work with the owner to make sure he was satisfied with it. That was the performance part. Then I asked each customer to tell a friend about my work. That was the pursue part.

"It worked out real well for me. I didn't hit 100% on referrals, but my business grew to the point where I had to get an assistant. Soon there were three of us and we started to clean carpets and other floors as well as windows. Later, I branched out into commercial buildings—my first one coming as a result of a referral by one of my home customers. I now have quite a large and successful operation. I don't mind telling you that I have done very well for myself all because of my system of doing good work and then getting my customers to tell others about me. When you do good work, the rest is easy. Nowadays, people appreciate that extra effort and they'll go out of their way to pass the word."

Perform and pursue. That could well be a motto for you to adopt in your own selling efforts. If you do a good job for your own customers and help them make money, they will tell others in your industry about you. Look what it did for Thorenson! After the class he was discussing his business with the professor in the latter's office. At one point during the conversation Thorenson stated that he had personally averaged $50,000 each year for the previous three years. That wasn't too bad for a man who started out with a sponge and bucket. But he had an idea and it worked for him! He put his customers to work to get more business for himself.

Customers are always looking for idea salesmen and are often guided by the experiences of their friends in the business. Your customers are like many football players. Off the field and out of the sales arena they are often close friends. When your buyers get together at industry meetings they sometimes do a lot of talking. Be sure what they say is helpful and not harmful to you.

There is one word that speaks volumes and you must at all costs avoid having it hooked onto you. That word is BUT. You have all heard it. "Jack is a good salesman, but . . . Tony has a good follow through, but . . . Hank is a real nice guy, but . . . " One little word, and once your customers start using it on you, you can forget about getting any help from your customers in talking your way to sales. You have to earn their confidence before they go out of their way to help you.

I have lunch frequently with Jim Clark, a successful insurance underwriter. He made an interesting observation not long ago. "There is a misconception among many insurance people that you have to have a lot of friends to be successful in this business. I say you have to have a lot of satisfied customers—they are the ones who will develop new business for you. If I had to depend on selling to my friends, I would get out of insurance. The only way to build volume is through satisfied customers and their referrals."

Perform and pursue; satisfied customers and referrals—they both have the same message. Mr. Thorenson and Jim Clark both used these skills to talk their way to successful sales. You can do the same.

HOW TO DRAW HELP FROM OTHERS WHOM YOU CONTACT EACH DAY

As you go about your business, you run across many people each day. You never know when one of them will help you: the newsboy on the corner; the man who parks your car; a desk clerk; a waitress; and many others. It doesn't cost you one red cent to smile and be pleasant to all of these people. When you least expect it they can give you information that will be helpful to you in talking your way to sales. It is unbelievable how kindness and pleasantness has a way of coming back to you.

Ed Kohler, the desk clerk at a hotel in my territory, told me when I checked in one evening that his wife had just presented him with a baby boy. I told my own wife about it and she sent a little present to them. She had met Kohler on a trip she made in the territory with me. You would have thought we had given them a new TV set! I never saw anyone so grateful for such a small consideration.

Some six months later I checked in at the hotel and Kohler remarked, "Must be something cooking. All of your competitors are in town. One of them brought his big boss with him and I heard him say something about trying to nail down the job before anyone else gets there."

I looked in the bar and sure enough, it looked like a floor covering convention. I knew they were all in town to try to get the order for a big school job on which Pat Jamison, one of the local flooring contractors, had the contract. I also knew that they would all be parked on the buyer's doorstep early the following morning.

I went to my room, picked up the phone and called Jamison at his home to make an early breakfast appointment with him at a restaurant on the other end of town. He agreed. I met him the following morning, got first crack at him, and got the order. It was a large job and cost of materials was $9,000.00. When I told him my competitors would be tearing down his door, Pat suggested we play nine holes of golf to give them a chance to leave town. He told me, "I hadn't quite made up my mind who I was going to give the order to, but your phone call last night decided the matter for me."

The whole point of this case story is that I never would have telephoned the customer had Kohler not told me about all my competitors being in town. I might have written the order without his help, but his tip-off made it easy for me. Those little bootees my wife sent certainly more than paid for themselves.

You never know when one of the people you contact in the course of your work will give you information or ideas that will help you talk your way to successful sales, so always be friendly with everyone and wear a smile instead of a scowl.

Jerry Stone, one of my salesmen, told me about a chain of events that certainly proved the value of being on good terms with everyone in the territory. He said, "I always eat in the coffee shop of a big restaurant operation in one of the towns in my territory. There is a waitress there who doesn't have a single brick out of place. All of the traveling men leave her good tips. One day she told Chuck Jones, a furniture salesman, that she had overheard the owner of the restaurant tell someone that he was going to remodel the entire restaurant and coffee shop. Chuck was a sharp operator so he approached the owner and got in on the ground floor by telling the owner he could save him a lot of money. And because of his knowledge of decoration and colors, Chuck sold a nice package. He told one of my good customers about the job and he got a contract for new floors, for which I received the order on our material. That little redhead sure got us all some nice business."

Chuck knew the importance of being nice to others, even though they had no relationship with his business. Because he had treated the waitress like a human being (in addition to being generous with tips), she responded by giving him information that enabled him to talk his way to a successful sale. And in the process she made it possible for Jerry to pick up a nice order for the floor covering. An order for $2,000.00 was put in his lap all because a furniture salesman had been kind to a waitress. Not a large order to be sure, but it was pure gravy for Jerry.

I am not minimizing the importance of your buyers. Without their support you can't write business. However, never overlook or forget others who can help you talk your way to successful selling: 1) the people around the buyer; 2) the people in your own company; 3) salespersons handling non-related products; 4) your other customers; and 5) other people you contact each day. Put them all to work for you. Get them on your side and you'll be kept busy writing orders.

5

HOW TO MAKE MORE SALES BY INCREASING YOUR SELLING TIME

Not a single day passes without hearing somebody say, "I wish there were more time. There just aren't enough hours in the day to accomplish the things I want to do." That's utter nonsense! There will never be any more time. There are exactly twenty-four hours in each day, and there is absolutely nothing that you and I or anyone else can do to change it. The trouble with most people, including salespersons, is that they don't make the most of that time. They are usually victims of their own procrastination. The problem is not the lack of time—it is the misuse of time.

If you are an average salesperson, you get up in the morning after a night of sleep, get dressed, eat your breakfast, get in your car to start your day's work, take time out for lunch, get home or back to the hotel around six, have dinner, spend the evening in relaxation and entertainment, and finally hit the sack. You do this day in and day out without giving any thought to the time you actually devote to each of your activities during a twenty-four hour period.

Let me stop for a moment and suppose that you are selling golf equipment to pro shops and other retail outlets, or you are selling a line of cosmetics, or automobile parts; or any one of hundreds of thousands of items that are manufactured and distributed every hour and day of the year. Then let me ask you some simple questions. How much time of your twenty-four hours do you actually devote to selling? Have you ever stopped to consider how many minutes each day you spend with your buyers? Have you ever made an analysis of your day on a minute-to-minute basis to ascertain exactly what you are doing with your time? If you have never done so, and decide to make such an analysis, you may be in for a big surprise. I can safely predict that you are spending much less time with your buyers than you think.

HOW TO DETERMINE THE TIME YOU DEVOTE TO SELLING

This book is primarily concerned with selling skills and techniques that will help you talk your way to more sales. I feel that it is of equal importance that you explore the possibilities and opportunities to create more selling time for yourself. Ask the average salesperson how his day breaks down and it's more than likely that you'll get an answer similar to the following: "I spend eight hours sleeping, eight hours working, and eight hours relaxing and enjoying life." Wrong! It isn't that simple. I submit a contrary opinion which states that you spend much less than eight hours in your work. I know, because I have made time studies of my own daily activities in the past and I have seen those of other salespersons. There is no way that a salesperson can put in an average of eight hours a day in actual selling. It is, therefore, of extreme importance to you that you know how much time you *are* devoting each day to selling. Your own time, and not other people's time, is the only thing that matters. Don't worry about the other fellow—just make certain you aren't a timewaster.

There are probably other ways to do it, but the simplest and most obvious procedure to check yourself is to take your own twenty-four hour day and keep a record hour-by-hour, half hour-by-half hour, and then refine it even further on a minute-to-minute basis. I suggest that you keep a daily record of your time for a period of at least one month so you can establish a mean or average. Anything less wouldn't be meaningful. It will take a little effort and patience, but it's well worth it.

Selling is different from other professions in that salespersons for the most part, have more freedom—they have a greater choice and more latitude in determining how to utilize their time. But there is danger in not knowing how to use that freedom. Most people—factory workers, doctors, lawyers, office workers, etc.—are tied down to schedules that are actually set up for them by others. Some are on very rigid working hours. Many even have to punch a clock. Not so with the salesperson. You establish your own schedule and make your own determination as to how you are going to use your time. It becomes doubly important therefore, that you exercise care in the manner in which you orchestrate your daily program.

It would be difficult to try to average out time for all salespersons because of the wide variety of products, differences in types of businesses, and variances in kinds of territories. It is impossible for me to tell you how much time you are, or should be, devoting to selling. Only you can determine this for yourself. All I can do is to urge you to find out for yourself how your day breaks down and suggest a way to go about doing it.

The Case of Jason McKittrick

I feel that the experience of one man who made a daily analysis of his time might be helpful. It can be a comparison guideline for you. Jason McKittrick is representative of a great many salespersons. He was a manufacturer's representative handling a line of kitchen stools and patio furniture, along with other small items. Most of his customers were furniture specialty shops and department stores. His territory was in an outlying area, some one hundred miles from a metropolis.

Jason felt that he wasn't getting the most out of time that was available to him, so he decided to make a study each day for one month to determine exactly how much time he was devoting to selling. He actually made the study for six weeks and came up with the following breakdown of an average twenty-four hour day:

Time devoted to sleep	8 hours
Time devoted to eating (includes shaving and dressing in the morning)	3 hours
Time devoted to travel	2½ hours
Time devoted to paper work and complaints	1 hour
Time devoted to relaxation and recreation	4½ hours
Time devoted to work	5 hours
TOTAL	24 hours

On the face of it, that doesn't seem too bad. You can accomplish a lot working five hours each day. However, it didn't quite come out that way for Jason. He averaged nine calls each day, which meant that he was devoting approximately one half hour to each call. However, that half hour was not all spent in actual selling. After diluting the half hour by time used up waiting for the buyer, interruptions such as telephone calls, and people asking questions, the study showed that only *ten to fifteen minutes* were actually spent with the buyer. On the basis of nine calls a day, this meant that Jason was spending an average of two hours each day in actual selling.

Jason realized that just making an analysis of his time would prove to be worthless unless he used the information and took steps to try to improve his situation. There was a profitable small line of sundry items that he was eager to add to what he already had, but he had to make sure he could handle it. Jason then set out to find ways to cut down on non-productive time. The result was that he did find the time and was able to take on the additional product line by making two simple adjustments in his daily schedule, as follows:

*Time devoted to sleep	7½ hours
Time devoted to eating (including shaving and dressing)	3 hours
*Time devoted to travel	2 hours
Time devoted to paper work and complaints	1 hour
Time devoted to relaxation and recreation	4½ hours
Time devoted to work	6 hours
TOTAL	24 hours

Jason found *weak spots in his sleeping time and in his travel time and made the necessary adjustments to pick up an extra hour each day for work. He took on the new line of products and increased his commissions $1600 the first year. As he told a friend, "That extra half hour of sleep, which I really didn't need, sure was costing me an awful lot of money!"

One interesting and significant thing about Jason's new allocation of time was that he picked up the extra hour each day by decreasing only two non-productive areas. It is worth noting that he didn't alter the time devoted to eating, and to relaxation and recreation.

This focuses attention on a very important point. If you expect to put out all you can while working, it is imperative that you take time off to mentally and physically prepare yourself so you can do a 100% job. Remember that a boxer has to pull back his arm to a state of rest before he can throw a punch at his opponent. It's the same with a hard-hitting salesperson. Eating properly and getting relaxation and recreation each day are as important segments of know-how as is the actual work itself.

Some people seem to believe that having fun and taking time for recreation and relaxation constitute an act of stealing on the job. I once overheard a conversation between two salesmen who were complaining about the fact that their sales manager was a slave driver. One commented, "Even when I'm home in bed with my wife he makes me feel I'm cheating on the company." Sounds rather far fetched but one thing is sure—that sales manager isn't going to get the most out of his salespersons.

If you are constantly worn out and dragging your heels you can't possibly enjoy your work, and when you are not happy with what you are doing, you won't do an effective job. Jason realized this, and as a result, he was able to make adjustments without infringing on his "fun time." It was well worth the effort because he was able to take on the additional line of sundries and add to his income.

WHAT YOU CAN DO TO CREATE MORE SELLING TIME

Your own breakdown of your daily activities may not correspond exactly with Jason's situation, but I don't think you will be too far off. The important thing is that you make your own study and then, if you are not satisfied with the amount of time you are devoting to selling, try to do something about it by begging, borrowing, and stealing from the non-productive moments of your day.

How You Can Cut Down On Travel Time

Not long ago I asked the head of an insurance agency, "How much time do your underwriters devote to travel each day in their cars?" When he scratched his head and hesitated, I continued, "Would you believe two and a half hours day in and day out?"

He snapped back, "That's ridiculous! They don't spend near that amount of time on the road!"

After we had kicked the subject around for over an hour, he finally agreed. "Well, if you are talking about an average based on a month, I guess you are right. Two and half hours! It never dawned on me that it would come to that! It's sure a lot of wasted time, but I don't know what can be done about it."

Actually there is something you can do about the amount of time you spend in your car. It all boils down to better scheduling. Since we all seem to be living on wheels, it behooves us to use every means we can think of to cut down on our travel time. Please remember that I am talking about averages. It is quite possible that your type of work is an exception and you therefore are not faced with this problem. If that is true, you are indeed fortunate.

In this era of freeways and crowded streets, one way you can cut down on your travel time is to schedule your work so you hit the freeways and surface streets at off hours. Sitting in a jammed up traffic situation not only kills valuable time, but is also aggravating to your nerves and disposition. After stewing for an hour, stalled on a freeway, you can't possibly be at your best on your next call.

In addition to scheduling your time so you don't hit the freeways at a bad hour, it might be well to take a good long look at the routing of your calls on customers. We all develop habits of doing things in a certain routine way, which in itself is not proof that what we are doing is best for us. Every moment saved in travel can be turned into more time for selling, so anything you can do to lessen travel time will assure more money for you.

Rule: You need your car to get around, but don't waste time in it.

How You Can Cut Down On Paper Work And Red Tape

I recently attended a luncheon honoring a friend who was retiring from his company after almost thirty-five years of service.

Seated next to me was the regional manager of his firm. Somehow we got on the subject of paper work.

He exclaimed, "I never saw anything like it. The home office snows us with bulletins, sales notices, letters, etc. I spend half my time wading through them. We must own a paper factory somewhere."

I asked, "How do your salesmen handle their paper work?"

He smiled and answered, "That used to be a problem, but I found a solution that works very well. Instead of their coming into the office any time during the week to pick up their stuff, we now have a set rule. They all come in for lunch at 12:30 every Friday, after which they return to the office to do their paper work. In the long run this saves a lot of time. If anything important comes up during the week, I know where to reach them because they all submit weekly schedules each Friday afternoon. Unless something of an emergency nature arises, the men all know they are not to come to the office any day other then Friday."

When I suggested that the weekly gatherings might turn into bull sessions he admitted, "One danger in having them all in the office at the same time is that they'll want to do a lot of yakking and not get their work done. As soon as we all come in from lunch, however, the silence sign goes up and stays up until they're all finished. Then they can sit around and swap lies and throw the bull, as all salesmen are prone to do." That's one way to handle paper work. If properly controlled it can save a lot of time. Try it—perhaps it is an answer for you. Make it a practice to go to your office on a set day at a fixed time.

Going to the office on a specific day each week will save a lot of time. Actually, this is a self-discipline that all salespersons need. As much as they hate paper work, there is something about their desk in the office that seems to attract them like a magnet. You all have your own lists of famous last words. At the top of my own list I place those fatal words you and many salespersons have probably used, "I think I'll pop by the office for a couple of minutes to pick up a few things!" Chances are excellent that you'll stay in the office the rest of the day! There are always delays, interruptions, telephone calls and other things to do that will keep you there. There is no such thing as "popping by the office for a few minutes." It's impossible, and the sad thing about it is that most salespersons know it.

When it's snowing or raining outside, or it's so hot you can fry eggs on the hood of your car, it's a real temptation to get out of it and find an excuse to get to the office sanctuary where it is nice and warm, or cool, as the case may be. Besides, "I can use the phone to call my customers—they'll understand"; or "There are some letters I should get off and I'm behind on my bulletins"; or I've got to get those samples straightened out." Be very careful! This business of dropping by the office can be habit forming and it can raise havoc with all of your time studies, schedules, and territorial plans.

Jimmy Bandole, a top salesperson for an auto parts wholesaler, once said, "When the weather is lousy, I know all of my competitors are taking cover somewhere. I keep going and have things all to myself. Even the buyers are glad to see me coming in. It's good news when I wake up in the morning and see that it's snowing or pouring down buckets. I get out there among 'em. I can't make any money sitting on my duff in the office—or at a bar somewhere, like so many other guys do."

Every salesperson has the responsibility of deciding what he is going to do with his time. Whatever you do, I urge you to stay away from the office unless it is absolutely necessary for you to go there.

One salesman I knew said, "I always keep a file of bulletins and sales notices in my sales case. When I am sitting, waiting to see a buyer, I pull them out and start reading. It's a lot better than just sitting and stewing, and it also saves a lot of time in getting my paper work done. Besides, it keeps me from getting trapped in the office." You might try this yourself—it could save you a lot of valuable time.

Axiom: You make your money selling—not pushing papers.

Change Your Sleeping Habits To Increase Your Selling Time

Many people will tell you that they require eight or nine hours sleep each night. Are they sure about that? Perhaps they are right, but a well-known doctor once submitted a contrary opinion when he suggested that a lot of people sleep themselves stupid, and they would be much better off if they spent less time in bed. The implication here is that too much sleep is actually harmful to the individual.

There are many who follow the precepts of Benjamin Franklin for the assurance that going to bed early and arising early makes a man healthy, wealthy and wise. This may sound like a good schedule, but as one highly successful salesman once said many years ago, he could not recall a single man who had acquired health, wealth or wisdom by following this rule. And there were Edison, Churchill, Dupont, and countless others who contradicted it.

Sleep is certainly necessary, but getting too much sleep can become a habit. It is a luxury that a salesperson cannot afford! Actually, it is a matter of self discipline. You form your own sleeping pattern and in your own mind are convinced how many hours you require each night. Perhaps by doing some experimenting you will find out that you are wrong, and that in reality you do not require as much sleep as you think you do.

One salesman once said, "I used to feel that eight hours of sleep was a must for me. When I learned from others that they got along on seven hours, I set out to experiment by deliberately fluctuating my time for sleep. I quickly discovered that six hours was not enough. I soon learned that anything over seven hours and a half was time wasted. So you see, just by learning from others I was able to gain a half hour of time that I could put to good use in my selling."

Try experimenting. Even if you can reduce your sleeping time as little as fifteen minutes every night, your effort will be worthwhile. Those little bonus moments can mean more $$$$'s in your pocket.

Use Appointments To Increase Your Selling Time

Some salespersons make it a practice to send post cards to their customers prior to making a trip in the territory. One I knew had a printed postcard, which he filled in by hand and sent every Friday afternoon for the following week:

> Dear__________
>
> I will be in your area next week and expect to call on you at approximately ________________________.
>
> I look forward to seeing you again.
>
> ________________

I asked him if these cards were effective and was rather surprised at the definiteness of his answer.

He exclaimed, "I wouldn't miss sending them for anything! My customers really like knowing when I will be there. It not only saves me a lot of time, but it saves them time. Furthermore, it is a form of self discipline for me—makes me stick to my schedule. If I get a little behind in my schedule, you'd be surprised how quick they are to remind me of it. They actually do pay attention to those cards."

While these cards are not actually appointments, they do in a sense have the same effect because the buyers who receive them know when to expect the salesperson who sent them. If your work and your territory are such that you can use this technique of sending advance cards, it would be extremely worthwhile for you to develop such a program. Experience of others who have used them would tend to prove that they are conducive to saving time.

There are some buyers with whom it is *mandatory* for you to make an appointment if you expect to see them. This is no guarantee that you won't have to wait after you arrive at their office but it does constitute an advance arrangement that you will be seen by the buyer. In some lines of selling it is impossible to make appointments with your buyer. You just have to take your chances on catching him in and being able to talk to him. If it looks like you will have a long wait before you have a chance to see him, don't waste time sitting. Tell his secretary you'll be back later and go on your way. You'll save time for yourself, and you'll also keep him from feeling that you are pushing him.

WHAT OTHERS HAVE DONE TO EVALUATE THEIR TIME

Benjamin Franklin is best known as a statesman, scientist, inventor, writer, and philosopher. He was also a great salesman. Many of his contributions to our country stemmed from his capacity to understand the desires and needs of others, along with the know-how to use the skills and techniques that are marks of a good salesperson. One has only to read history to learn what a profound effect his great salesmanship had on the internal affairs as well as the international relations of this nation.

It is not only interesting, but significant, that Dr. Franklin was very methodical in the allocation of his time each day: An early riser, he laid out his plans for the day ahead, in which he devoted eight hours to his work, not including time out for lunch. At the end of his work day he always reviewed what he had accomplished. Then, after supper, he indulged in conversation, music, or other relaxation. He diligently adhered to this daily program.

Because Dr. Franklin was so successful in so many diversified fields of endeavor, it is well that we take a close look to ascertain what we, as salespersons, can learn from him. To be sure, he didn't have freeways, automobile traffic, TV, and a myriad of other modern devices to cope with, but he understood the value of time and the importance of making plans for using it to advantage. Looking at his daily procedure, we come up with a simple formula that can be beneficially put to use by any salesperson: (1) plan, (2) work, (3) evaluate.

We discuss the importance of planning your work and working your plan later in the book (Chapter 9). It is the third part of the formula that we are concerned with at this point. So you made your plans and tried to work them during your day! Do you ever stop at the end of the day to review what you have done? Do you pick up the good things you did so you can repeat them? Are you aware of what you did wrong so you can avoid making the same mistakes again? Fifteen minutes spent each evening in going over your day may well be the most meaningful time you put in on your twenty-four hours. Evaluate! Don't leave it out of your daily schedule.

I recently discussed the subject of the proper use of time with the general sales manager of a large corporation. He told me, "There is no question in my mind that most salesmen can increase their output ten percent by cutting out a lot of nonsensical wasted time. I go over daily schedules periodically with each of my men and together we pick out any flaws. I learned early, when I was a beginner salesman, that wasted time can be costly. It's easy to fall into the trap of procrastination, but it is through having an awareness of time that this pitfall can be avoided. The only way to do this is to know what you are doing each hour of the day."

This man must have known what he was talking about because he was in the $70,000 a year income bracket.

I knew one corporation president who made it a practice to never see anyone in his office until eleven each morning. He told me, "I am one of those 'morning people' and need those three hours from eight to eleven each day to catch up on reports and formulate plans. My people know it and leave me alone. I wouldn't get a damned thing accomplished if I didn't adhere to this set routine."

Jack Kitters, an account executive in a large investment house in the West, made an interesting observation, "When you stop to realize it, all of us in this business are selling the same product. 1000 shares of General Motors, IBM, Exxon—you name it—they're all the same, regardless of who you buy them from. With so many reputable firms to pick from in the business, the whole thing boils down to the individual salesman and what he does with his time. You have to be in your office when the board is open, but after that you've got a lot of time to either waste or put to work for you. After I have taken care of the business of my customers, I then set out to devote two hours each day trying to drum up new business. This is a *must* for me. I never deviate from this set program even though at times results are not what I hope for. In the long run, however, it pays off."

It did pay off for Kitters, to the tune of $50,000 a year.

We all have one thing in common, from the man who washes dishes to the President of the United States. We all have twenty-four hours in each day—no more, no less. I have observed that the higher up the ladder you climb, the more important allocation of time becomes. Conversely, those who learn how to apportion their time early in their careers seem to be the ones who make it to the top. Be sure you allow enough time each day for the application of your know-how and selling skills and techniques.

6

HOW NOT TO TALK YOUR WAY TO SUCCESS IN SELLING

The songwriter knew what he was saying when he admonished us to "accentuate the positive and eliminate the negative." He must have been a salesman at one time in his life because his advice is so applicable to selling. Many salespersons concentrate on the positives when talking their way to sales, but they often fail to eliminate the negatives. The result is that their overall effectiveness becomes watered down. Some persist in making errors of omission and commission without realizing what they are doing.

It is significant, therefore, that this "how not to" chapter is included in this book. It would be impossible to include all of the "don't's" of selling. An entire book could be written on that subject alone. I have singled out a number of selling negatives that are observed every day in the marketplace, with warnings and suggestions concerning each. Perhaps you will find some areas where you have been guilty and can take immediate steps to eliminate your own negatives for better selling.

DON'T MAKE PROMISES YOU CAN'T KEEP

How well do you keep your promises? Can you be depended upon to do what you say you will do, or are you quick to make a promise but slow to carry it out. Don't forget that to most people, a promise is serious business—it is a verbal contract. Plans are often made on the promises of others.

Little promises that are broken can be a source of great irritation. The promise of a woman to bring a salad to a pot luck dinner, and she arrives empty handed. You telephone someone who tells you, "Sorry, I can't talk right now. I'll call you back shortly," and three hours later you are still waiting for his return call. A jeweler promises to clean your watch and have it ready for you on Friday, and you go out of your way to pick it up only to be casually advised that it won't be ready until Monday. Promises, promises, promises! Perhaps people can get by with broken promises on the mashed potato circuit, but it is a definite "no-no" in selling.

Say What You Mean And Mean What You Say

Don't ever make a promise just to get an order or to get a buyer off your back when you have no intention of keeping it. Don't count on his forgetting about it. Sooner or later the law of averages will catch up with you. When that happens you will have an unhappy customer—the creation of your own lack of responsibility and sincerity. Don't ever let yourself get caught in that trap.

One salesman did. Dan Rinker sold electronic devices, tape recorders and cameras. His company had just made a connection as distributors for a new imported line of tape recorders which was a quality product at a low cost. Anxious to get a large order from the most important outlet in town, he promised the buyer that he would give him an exclusive on the line for six months. He got the order. Then he got greedy. About a month later he sold the same line to two other dealers in town. It wasn't long before the first dealer heard about it and things really hit the fan! Rinker not only lost a customer, but he also lost about $25,000 worth of business per year. Stupid, you say? Of course, but believe it or not, it happens every day!

It's easy to make a promise to your buyer that you know you can't possibly keep, but it's more difficult to explain it to him.

I had a customer come storming into my office one morning, red faced and obviously extremely upset about something. Tom Harris, one of our salesmen, had promised to get him a roll of a particular pattern that was completely sold out, with no stock at the wholesalers, and with an availability date almost two months in the future. On the basis of the promise, the customer had sold the pattern to one of his good consumers who proceeded to have her kitchen repainted to match the new pattern. When she was advised that there would be a delay of over two months, she blew her stack! She threatened to take him and our company to court. After considerable time and expense we were able to locate sufficient yardage to do the job from a dealer in another state, and got a lot of frayed nerves settled down. Needless to say, Tom learned quite a lesson on the subject of making a promise without being sure that he could produce. He paid for his eagerness to write an order by having many anxious hours.

Follow Through Or Foul Up

When you make a promise to one of your customers, follow through and make sure that all bases are covered. You can never assume that others will do what they are supposed to do, so it is up to you to stay on top of the situation and make certain that there are no slip-ups. Many salespersons are sincere when they make promises but fall down because they don't follow through. Just weaken one link in a chain of action necessary to carry out a promise and you'll have a real foul-up on your hands.

It's a long route from your customer's place of business, to the person who writes up the order in your office, to your credit department for approval, to the stock clerk for filling the order, to the shipping clerk who sees to it that the order is shipped according to instructions. If any one of these slips up or makes a mistake, your customer will hold *you* responsible. It is therefore up to you when you make a promise to make sure there are no breakdowns.

Keep Your Appointments And Keep Peace

It is an unforgivable business sin to make an appointment with a customer for a specific time and then fail to show up. This not only shows a complete lack of concern for others but is a sure sign of irresponsibility. You can get yourself into a lot of trouble if you don't take appointments seriously. There are two **rules** you must follow at all times:

1. Never make an appointment unless you are sure you can keep it.
2. If something comes up that makes it impossible to keep your appointment, be sure to notify the one who is expecting you and explain the circumstances.

Appointments and promises are in the same ballpark. You won't score if you fail to keep them.

Wayne Doser, a life insurance underwriter, can attest to the truth of these two rules. He had a program worked out for life insurance for a client and had a firm appointment to see him on a Monday morning. Several salesmen from other companies were after this nice policy. Doser was involved in an automobile accident Sunday morning resulting in his hospitalization with a broken leg. He knew that it was impossible to see his client the next day so he proceeded to forget about the appointment. Even though the client later heard about Doser's accident and felt badly about it, he was burned up at the time because he hadn't been notified that the appointment would have to be cancelled. The client had cancelled out two other engagements to meet with Doser. The result: Doser lost a $100,000 policy.

QUIT KNOCKING YOUR COMPETITORS AND THEIR PRODUCTS

Spend an evening watching TV and what do you see and hear on many commercials? "Our fried chicken tastes better than Cackle Chicken; Our soap cleans whiter than Slippery Soap; Our soft drink is chosen by most people over Hoola Coola; Our car gets better mileage than the Super Dooper; Our tires last longer than the Flatt Tire." All of these commercials and many others are playing the *comparison game*.

This kind of selling is not limited to TV commercials. You also see it in newspaper and magazine advertising. It is little wonder, therefore, that salespersons use the same technique in their own selling efforts. Mine is a contrary opinion. I don't believe in that kind of selling. I submit that whatever you are selling you should sell it on its own merits. Forget about your competition. Why give them free exposure time and space? Why take a chance on irritating a customer who reacts negatively to comparison selling?

A Knock Can Be A Boost

The trouble with comparison selling is that it eventually degenerates into the *knocking game*. I have actually seen a salesperson carrying samples of a competitive line to try to prove the superiority of his own product. Throwing rocks at competitors may help you make sales with some customers, but I have found that most buyers actually resent it.

I know of one expensive car that was bought because the salesman for a competitive make knocked it. The buyer had been on the fence as to which make to buy but the "knocker" decided the matter for him and in the process, lost a $14,000 sale.

Step on the other side of the fence for a moment and ask yourself how you react when you are buying something and the salesperson, trying to sell a particular product, knocks others. My own inclination is to learn more about the product being run down.

Many football coaches keep their players away from newsmen on the eve of a big game for fear that they will make some derogatory remarks concerning the quality of their opposition. Do you know what happens if something like that should appear in the newspaper? It goes right up in the center of the bulletin board in the opposing team's locker room! Games have been won and lost because some big mouth was stupid enough to make a remark that riled up a whole team into a "let's get those slobs" crusade.

The same thing can happen to you. If you have good knowledge of your own product and the know-how to sell it, why bring your competitors into your act? Let them do the knocking. Let them give you free advertising! Let them help you talk your way to sales, but don't give them any assistance!

Don't Insult Your Buyer's Intelligence

Your buyer is in business to make money and he will buy whatever in his own judgment will do the best job for him. When he buys merchandise from your competitors, you may not agree with his having done so, but that gives you no right to question his decision. Usually when your buyer puts in competitive merchandise it is you who has fallen down on the job somewhere along the line.

Sim Harper, a paper products salesman, lost a good customer because he was indiscreet. He walked into a customer's store one day just as the warehousemen were bringing in some new competitive merchandise. Sim was so upset he lost his cool. He sneeringly remarked to the buyer, "How come you're putting in that junk? They must be giving it to you on consignment—you surely didn't *buy* it!"

He paid dearly for his remark. He had insulted the buyer's intelligence and from that point forward his volume with that customer fell off. Sim lost $1000.00 each year in commissions because of his stupidity.

If you ever bump into a situation where one of your competitors has outflanked you, your solution is not to knock his merchandise or question your buyer's judgment, but to double your own efforts and use the skills and techniques at your disposal to sell your own product and prevent it from happening again.

Axiom: when you throw rocks at others you run the risk of catching a ricochet in your own teeth.

DON'T GET TOO INTIMATE WITH YOUR BUYERS

This is probably another contrary opinion, but I am satisfied from personal experience and observation that it's a dangerous practice to become too friendly with your buyer. I thoroughly advocate a friendly seller-buyer association, but when your relationship reaches a point where there are emotional involvements, then you have lost your effectiveness as a salesperson. When that happens it's time to call in the clowns.

You cannot buy business through friendship, particularly when it is nothing more than a social masquerade devised to achieve your own selfish aims. Getting "thick" with your buyer may work for a while, but sooner or later it will catch up with you and your paper house will go up in flames, sparked by some disagreement. When you disagree with a buyer, it is on a business basis; when you disagree with a close friend, it is on a personal basis. Close friendship and business are two things that just don't go together and it is a wise salesperson who doesn't try to mix them.

You may start out gaining more business by developing a close personal relationship with your buyer, but eventually he will turn the tables on you. His chief objective is to make a profit—never forget that! He will, therefore, use every available weapon to achieve that objective, even if he has to put your friendship on the block to do it. These may seem to be hard cold words, but they have been given the stamp of approval by many who have had unfortunate experiences.

One was Mike Adair, a salesman for a stationery supply company. He made the mistake of starting to get too personally involved with a major customer. In the beginning, everybody was happy, including the customer. Mike never came to town without dining with the family. He even started to go on dates with their daughter. Everything was great. Business was good and they were all having an enjoyable time. That is, until Mike started to hear the sound of wedding bells growing louder and louder. He backed off before things got too "sticky." He began to cool off, much to the chagrin of the entire family. The buyer's friendship turned to hatred and the "unwelcome sign" was put up for the salesman. From that point on the buyer bought only what he had to buy from Mike who later confessed to a friend, "How stupid can a guy get? That girl cost me darn near $1300.00 a year in commissions."

This is an extreme case, of course, but it points up the danger of getting too involved with the buyer's life. There certainly isn't anything wrong with going with him to a football game now and then to watch his son play, or to take him and his wife out for dinner. But when it becomes a habit and he expects you to do it, then you are swimming upstream in dangerous waters. Get out before it is too late and you drown in complications.

Knowing your buyer and being able to recognize all of the defense weapons in his arsenal is one thing. But when you permit a friendly seller-buyer relationship to degenerate into an intimate personal relationship, then he will include a new weapon in his arsenal—demands that only one friend can make on another.

Axiom: keep your buyer at arm's length and you'll keep your buyer.

DON'T BE A CHRONIC COMPLAINER

Selling can sometimes get pretty rough. The marketplace is exacting in the demands it makes on you, and there is no concession given to carelessness or halfheartedness. Despite how hard you try to avoid them you will make mistakes, and some of them can really hurt. However, I agree with the poet who once said, "The mistakes which make us men are better than the accuracies that keep us children." It is how you recover from your mistakes that determines what kind of a salesperson you truly are.

Nobody likes the guy who continually whines and says the cards are always stacked against him. Don't be a poor loser. If you get knocked out of a sale because you either made a mistake or someone outsold you, then, instead of crying about it, you should get yourself better prepared for the next time around.

Don't Yell At The Carrots

You can't make carrots grow by yelling at them. Likewise, you can't change things by constantly complaining about them. One of the worst things a salesperson can do is complain to his buyer about his job, his company, or his domestic problems.

At an industry meeting, the speaker told about an experience on this subject. He commented, "A buyer once asked me if I could intercede with the management of one of my distributors to have a different man assigned to his account. The salesman was always complaining about something and the buyer just didn't like it. He protested, 'The guy always moans to me about how underpaid he is, and how tough it is for him to make ends meet at home because his old lady is so extravagant. I'm getting sick of listening to him. No wonder everybody calls him *Moaner*.'''

Your buyers aren't interested in listening to your problems or your tale of woe. They usually have enough of their own. If you aren't happy with your company and think you are not being fairly treated, the person to go to is your boss—not your buyers. Don't be a nuisance salesperson. Keep your problems to yourself. Don't yell at the carrots.

Don't Spend Too Much Time At The Wailing Wall

Whether you like it or not, you have to submit to certain rules and regulations in all of your activities. That is not to say, however, that in abiding by the law and rules of the game you have to forfeit your own individuality. It's up to you if you are to be a winner or a loser, but you'll never make it if you are a chronic complainer.

Don't be an "establishment bucker." There are some who always carry a chip on their shoulders. They resent rules and regulations. Nothing is ever right. "Daylight savings is for the birds; The fifty-five mile an hour speed limit is ridiculous; They can't keep me from running my dog on the beach; The brass at the home office are a bunch of idiots—they don't know what they are doing; Our prices are too high; I have a lousy territory; They always give me the tough accounts; etc., etc." These dissidents are always making waves because they resent authority. It's little wonder that so many of them fail.

There are two good **rules** to follow at all times:

1. Don't be a chronic complainer. Learn to roll with the

punches. Don't let yourself get the reputation of being a constant complainer.

2. Respect your superiors. Most of them made it the hard way. They are human, too, and make mistakes, but when policies come down from "upstairs," follow them until they are proven to be wrong. Remember, there is only *one* quarterback calling the signals.

NEVER TRY TO IMPRESS YOUR BUYER WITH YOUR KNOWLEDGE

It is important that you remember that you are a source of information as well as a source of supply for your buyers, but don't overdo it. He does need your help, but don't go on an ego trip and try to impress him by showing him how smart you are. It might backfire on you. If you "talk down" to your buyer, he will shift into reverse gear and back away from you. No one wants to be reminded that he is inferior, so you are scratching a very sensitive spot if he gets the feeling that you are trying to put on the superiority act.

Don't Be A Textbook Thinker

One of the weakest breeds of salespersons is the textbook thinker. He is short on selling skills and techniques, but can quote verbatim the contents of bulletins and sales notices from the home office. He knows exactly how his product is made and can readily recite all of the technicalities involved in its manufacture. He can tell the buyer how much glue and paper, or how many nails and feet of lumber are required for the packaging of his product, and he can snap off weights and dimensions without blinking an eye. But he is light on know-how and the use of selling skills and techniques. He would get a straight A in the classroom, but in the school of hard knocks, he is lucky to get a passing grade.

I once had a young salesman named Jerry Clayton, who had just finished his sales training course at the factory. He was loaded with information and knowledge concerning how our products were manufactured, and was extremely eager to share it with the customers in his territory. One day he was giving "the works" to one of our seasoned customers. It was quite a dissertation on manufacturing processes, and Jerry thought he was really coming through to the buyer until he was told, "Look, I don't care how your stuff is made. All I care about is how much it costs, how good it is, and how much money I can make on it!" I am sure that this was the last time Jerry tried to impress anyone with his knowledge. The buyer had done an excellent job of sticking a pin in his ego balloon.

I'm not suggesting for one moment that it is not necessary for you to have technical knowledge concerning your product. What I am saying is that it should never be used to impress your buyers. They are much more interested in what it can do for them—not in how it is made. This is just another case of pinpointing the importance of always having the buyers' viewpoint. When you are trying to impress your buyer with your technical knowledge, you are using the "I" approach; when you discuss his market potential, stock controls, dollar investment, profitability, etc., you are using the "you" viewpoint. Which of these two would you be the more interested in if you were the buyer?

Don't Try To Impress Your Buyer With Your Education And Background

Never try to impress your buyer by using words that he doesn't understand. So you went to college and took a course in English! Who cares? People who didn't have an opportunity to go to college frequently resent those who did. Your buyers could be in this group. It behooves you, therefore, to exercise extreme care in learning about the formal educational background of each of your buyers.

Many successful buyers never saw the inside of a college—they came up the hard way and are proud of their accomplishments.

Don't give them the "When I was in college . . ." bit. It will go over with them like a lead balloon. A college degree itself is not a passport to success in selling, but you can use what it represents wisely. No one, least of all a buyer who didn't go to college, is interested in your prowess on the football field or in campus politics. All they care to hear about is how they can make a profit on the product you are trying to sell them.

Axiom: always be dignified, but never act superior.

DON'T BE CARELESS IN PERSONAL HABITS

Don't Blow Smoke

We have heard an awful lot about cigarette smoking during recent years, and people who previously never gave the subject any thought are now getting involved in this very personal and controversial matter. Smokers and non-smokers have taken strong positions on this issue. We even have "smoking" and "no smoking" sections on airplanes.

This book is not concerned with the morality of smoking, or whether it is or is not injurious to your health. If you choose to smoke, that's for *you* to decide. However, I submit that there are times and places when you shouldn't smoke. I am referring to your buyer's office. Some people don't like their office filled with smoke, while others can't tolerate cigarette smoke because of allergies. Pulling out and lighting a cigarette in some offices is a sure way to kill your sale.

If smoke gets in the eyes of certain buyers, your order has a good chance of blowing out the window. Think about that the next time you are tempted to reach for a cigarette.

Axiom: never smoke unless your buyer smokes first.

Drinking And Selling Don't Mix

If you want to drink that's your business. I have no intention of moralizing on the subject or discussing its health aspects. All I am concerned with is selling. Like many people, I enjoy a couple of cocktails before dinner after a hard day of work, but I consider it to be poor policy to drink during the day. It is appalling to see so many men and women "drinking" their lunch, and it is difficult to understand how they can operate at 100% efficiency in the afternoon. With some buyers, if they get one whiff of liquor on your breath, you are wasting your time trying to sell them anything. It's one sure way *not* to open your order book.

One young salesman reportedly told his manager that in his case it was quite okay for him to drink at noon, because he drank only vodka and no one could smell it on his breath. His boss, who knew that this salesman often imbibed a little too much, replied, "I'd rather you drink gin, so your customers will know you're drunk and not think you're stupid!"

A smart salesperson knows that mixing selling and drinking can sometimes be an explosive formula. If you have to drink at noon with an important customer, knock off the rest of the day. Don't expose yourself to other customers.

Axiom: mix your bourbon with soda—not selling.

Understate Your Dress

Throughout the years, I have noted that top salespersons are usually understated in their attire. Perhaps it is the "in" thing to wear "far out" clothes, but I question the propriety of a salesperson wearing them on the job. In my judgment, people who are ultra-extreme in their manner of dress usually have inferiority complexes. You can't afford to have that label pinned on you!

First impressions are often made by how we look, so what we wear becomes doubly important. What about your hair? Are your shoes always shined? How about your finger nails? Do you *look* the part of a salesperson? We can't all be Beau Brummels, and certainly many feel that they got gyped and would like to trade their faces and bodies in for a different model. However, the important thing, regardless of what the good Lord chose for you, is what you do with what you have to work with.

How you are dressed and how you are groomed can affect your morale. People who are careless in their appearance are usually careless and shabby in their thinking. If you don't agree that clothes can make a difference in how you feel, just put on a new suit, or a new dress, as the case may be, and I challenge you not to experience an uplift.

Axiom: look and act the part—look like a winner.

DON'T BE A GOSSIPMONGER

Just how gossip travels has never been resolved, but travel it does. One of its surest routes is through a channel you are familiar with—the salesperson. A peculiar characteristic of gossip is that for the most part it pertains to things that are negative.

Unfortunately, there is a little bit of the gossip in each of us. The majority, however, are gossip "typhoid Marys." They unwittingly spread rumors through carelessness in what they say, and really don't mean to do harm. They are quite different from the malicious spreaders of dirt who seem to get their kicks from watching others suffer.

If someone carries tales to you, listen if you can't resist, but *never* repeat it! One sure way to avoid gossip is to make it a rule to never knowingly say anything unkind or untrue about anyone. When you start dishing out false information, sooner or later it will come back to you like a boomerang.

The manager of a small appliance manufacturer told me about one of his salesmen. He said, "Dick was a good man. He knew our products and was a great salesman. But he was too darned nosey and he talked too much! You know the type—he always had to be the first with 'the word' on everything. I never saw anyone like him. He had his own private pipelines all over his territory; he even had people at the factory who fed him information. He was a real pro as a gossip. A joyful bearer of bad news, he was at his best when everyone felt that the roof was caving in. I finally had to let him go. It was too bad because I really liked him, but his big mouth kept getting us all into a lot of trouble." Dick lost a $20,000 a year job because he was a gossipmonger!"

People for the most part resent gossips—and don't forget, that includes your customers. If you ever get this handle put on you, your associates, your customers and everyone else will always be suspicious of you. If you expect to make it in the selling game, you cannot afford the dubious luxury of being known as a gossip.

Axiom: if your mouth spews out mud and slime, some day your own feet will slip in it.

NEVER USE THE CANNED PRESENTATION

If all of your buyers were exactly alike and if their business establishments were identical in every respect, selling would be easy. All you would have to do is take all the knowledge you have concerning your product, boil it down to a few words, and then memorize them. In short, you would be developing a "canned" presentation.

Fortunately, all of your buyers are not alike and neither are their places of business. If they were, there wouldn't be any need for salespersons because the "canned" pitch could be transmitted by a computer. Unfortunately, some salespersons actually sound like computers and it is quite obvious to their buyers that their presentation has been memorized.

While it is imperative that you know what you are going to talk about when you call on your buyer, it definitely doesn't imply that you must know in advance exactly how you are going to say it. There is a wide variation between sale presentations that are memorized, that are impromptu, and that are extemporaneous.

1. *The memorized pitch* is one that has been pre-written and then memorized, word for word. This is the "canned" presentation.
2. *The impromptu pitch* is one made on the spur of the moment, without any preparation.
3. *The extemporaneous pitch* is one where the material has been prepared but not memorized.

Successful salespersons use only the third—the extemporaneous presentation. Selling without any pre-planning and selling by over-planning and memorizing both fall short.

Earlier we mentioned several "lead in" phrases that you can use to start your presentation to the buyer. You are on safe ground to memorize these and keep them in your mind so you can use them when they fit in. What is dangerous is to plan in advance the exact words you will use during your entire presentation. When you do this you are not selling—you are simply "mouthing" information to the buyer. If he gets wise to you, he will quickly find ways to trip you up and throw you off your path. You are then at a loss for words because he has disrupted your talk plan.

Every salesperson has his arsenal full of pet phrases that have worked well for him. If properly used, they can add credence to your presentation, but the important thing is that you don't let them dominate it. Don't sound like a computer!

Axiom: always know what you are going to say—not how you will say it.

DON'T BE CARELESS WITH THE TRUTH

Many people "stretch" the truth without realizing what they are doing. They are basically honest and wouldn't think of deliberately saying or doing anything that even verged on dishonesty. Actually, there are only a few salespersons I have met throughout the years whom I would consider to be out and out dishonest. There isn't much you can do about these thieves except to avoid them. To be sure, there are wheeling and dealing hucksters in the selling game, just like there are quacks in the medical profession and shysters in the legal profession; but for the most part, you will find salespersons, doctors, lawyers and people in all walks of life, are basically honest.

This is for those salespersons who get a little careless about telling the absolute truth. They mean no harm, but they sometimes get carried away when they are hot on the trail of an order. They are not even conscious of the fact that they are skirting along the edge of dishonesty.

Don't Misrepresent Your Product

What guarantees do you have on your product—both written and implied? Are you fully prepared to back up your claim that your watches will continue to run after being inundated in water for an hour? How good is your warranty on your tires, your TV sets, your underwear, or whatever? Exactly what does it state?

Whatever product you may be selling, there are definitely two things you must know about it and the people who make it: (1) exactly what can be expected of its performance, and (2) will the maker back you up if the product does not comply with specifications and warranties? If the manufacturer lets them down, factory representatives can find themselves out in left field when products fail.

Once you know about your manufacturers' policies, then it is up to you to sell their product in accordance with their ground rules. When you start to stretch the facts and misrepresent what your product will do, you are asking for real trouble. When you over-sell the capabilities of your product, expecting to find loopholes to bail you out if you get into trouble—forget it! The buyer isn't going to pick up the tab for your stupidity! Besides, he is usually much smarter than you give him credit for, particularly when it comes to anything that costs him money and reduces his profit.

Gary Doberson lost a $22,000 a year job selling material handling equipment because he misrepresented what his lift trucks could do.

Wayne Cowper, a factory sales representative who represented several small clothing manufacturers, lost 25% of his income in one year when one of his sources of supply took their line away from him. Complaints coming to them from dealers indicated that Cowper had misrepresented their products.

Axiom: being honest may cost you some business now and then, but in the long run it will pay off for you.

Always Be Straightforward In Your Dealings

I once knew a lamp and table salesman named Ed Larnon who told me that he never left a copy of an order with a buyer. Since this was completely contrary to my own practice, I asked him why.

Ed replied, "It's very simple. If I leave a copy, the buyer knows exactly what he ordered and it wouldn't be possible for me to make any changes, like substituting on something if we didn't have an item in stock."

Ed was a deacon in his church, and if I were to have told him that what he was doing was dishonest, he would have resented it very much. It never occurred to him that he was doing anything wrong. His was a "righteous" dishonesty. It wasn't until Ed lost a good customer, after making substitutions on an order and getting caught doing it, that he discontinued his practice. When he lost that customer, commissions of $750 annually went down the drain. It was a costly lesson.

Don't try to "cute trick" your buyers like Ed did. When you play it straight you won't have to worry about what they will do. Always be forthright about your product, even though it hurts and you may lose the sale. I have said it before and I think it bears repeating here—your buyers for the most part are smart people. Don't try to cheat them. Follow this rule and you'll keep yourself out of a lot of trouble.

DON'T AGREE WITH YOUR BUYER WHEN HE TALKS NEGATIVELY ABOUT HIS COMPETITORS

This is one of those "traps" that a salesperson can get himself caught in—one from which it is extremely difficult to extricate himself. Many buyers are natural complainers and are constantly telling you how unscrupulous their competitors are. More than likely, those competitors are also your customers. Some buyers say nasty things about your other customers to "bait" you—just to see what you will say. Any negative remarks on your part are passed along to the other customers. When that happens you have a lot of explaining to do.

Have you ever stepped in between a husband and wife to try to settle a family quarrel? If you haven't, don't ever try it because you will be inviting trouble for yourself. The same thing applies to your customers. If you try to arbitrate any kind of a dispute between them, you are the one who will come up with the short end of the stick.

Whenever you run into a situation where one of your customers is hot under the collar because of something one of his competitors did, there is one basic **rule** for you to follow: keep your mouth shut! One word from you and you immediately become a "co-conspirator." If your customer persists in trying to get you to say something, simply tell him it is your policy never to discuss with anyone matters of disagreement between customers. Many otherwise intelligent salespersons have become victims of their own unguarded remarks made to one customer concerning another.

George Binner would gladly sit down with you for a couple of hours to extoll the virtues of keeping your mouth zipped shut whenever one of your customers starts talking about another. All George did was lose 30% of his business in one community in his territory when he agreed with one buyer who called another a "chiselling s.o.b." Naturally the first buyer couldn't wait to tell the other, who was so teed off at George that he threw his line out and refused to buy anything from him.

This happens every day, so always be on guard. George admitted afterwards that he was stupid, but he thought by agreeing with the buyer who called the other names, he would be making points with him. It backfired on him and he lost a customer.

Axiom: every word you say to one customer might be told to another—so be careful what you say.

NEVER USE THE POOR MOUTH OR SYMPATHY APPROACH

This section has to be included in this book, because it focuses attention on a very important aspect of selling. To come right to the point, there are some people involved in selling who shouldn't be in this line of work. They just aren't cut out for selling, and should get out of it. The real trouble is that they are not aware of this fact and go blundering their way along, hoping that some day all of the pieces will fall in place for them.

Meanwhile, they are guilty of doing everything possible to get an order, even to the point of appealing to the buyer's sympathy—

using a "*poor mouth*" *approach*. When you reach the point where you have to get business that way, it's time for you to throw away your sales case, get out of the game, and hang up your spikes. You're just not cut out to be a salesperson!

That does not mean, however, that your life has ended and there is no future for you. On the contrary, you can find a niche doing something else that will give you peace of mind and also enable you to be a success. I consider that one of the responsibilities of a good sales manager is to closely observe all of his salespersons to make certain that they are mentally qualified to engage in selling as their livelihood. If a salesperson doesn't have the capacity, then he should be told, so he can get into some other kind of work before he ruins his life.

I have known several people who failed in selling but became successful in other lines of work. A case in point concerns Don Darklee, one of our wholesaler salesmen. His sales manager related the story to me.

"Don was very personable, was a willing worker, had excellent product knowledge, but always seemed to freeze up when talking to his buyers. We did all we could to help him, but when word came in that he was starting to use the sympathy approach on his buyers, I called him in for a long man-to-man discussion. After two hours of kicking the whole thing around, two points were clearly brought out: (1) Don didn't enjoy his work, and (2) he concluded that selling wasn't his cup of tea. Because I knew he was thorough in details and assiduously read and absorbed the contents of all bulletins and sales notices, I felt that he would make a good teacher.

"We both agreed that he should return to college, get a master's degree and go on to get teaching credentials. Don left our employ and I didn't hear from him for almost three years. It was heart-warming to read his letter, written from a small community in a state far away from the office. He went on to get his degree and became an instructor in economics in the local high school. Don said he couldn't be happier.

"It takes a lot of guts to face up to the fact that you are a failure in what you are doing, but it takes real courage to make a change. Don Darklee had what it takes and although I haven't heard about him for many years, I wouldn't be at all surprised if he is principal of that high school. He failed miserably as a salesperson, but is a success as an educator."

Unfortunately there are thousands of Don Darklees still carrying samples and sales cases trying to force a living in a type of work for which they are not qualified. Perhaps some of you who read this can take heart from the experience of Don Darklee. If you feel as he did, *now* is the time to get out and do something about it—unashamed, and happy that you can face up to it before you become forever locked up in a dungeon of unhappiness.

7

HOW TO LISTEN YOUR WAY TO SALES

The ability to talk is a prerequisite for any successful salesperson. Of equal significance is an awareness of the importance and necessity of being a good listener, and the wisdom of silence. Although your capacity to talk is usually the avenue by which you get orders, there are often situations when silence becomes the medium through which you can attain the results you are after. A Swedish proverb tells us to, "talk less and say more." Controlled talking is just as important to you as moderation in drinking and restraint in eating. Your mouth, ears, and eyes are some of the tools of your trade—use them wisely and carefully to help you talk your way to success in selling. Too much talking and not enough listening is dangerous, in that an imbalance can be created that will defeat your own objective—to produce sales.

THE IMPORTANCE OF KNOWING WHEN NOT TO TALK

I think it can be said without any question that the average salesperson is guilty of talking too much. Unfortunately they are not aware of this! They don't seem to realize that one of the secrets of good selling is knowing when to stop talking. Some salespersons bear down on the buyer without so much as pausing to take a deep breath. There is no way in the world that you can possibly know how you are scoring on your sale if your mouth is constantly moving. You have to force your buyer to talk—to enter the conversation—if you expect to talk your way to a successful sale. The only way you can do this is to stop talking, yourself, and listen!

Don't Get A Reputation For Being A Word "Drooler"

There was a salesman working for a distributor of home furnishings who had a reputation for being a big talker. The buyers in his territory, and his own associates as well, called him Motor Mouth. He had product knowledge, was fairly well versed in his business, but was only a less than average salesman in performance for the simple reason that he didn't know when to keep his big mouth shut. He talked his way *out* of as many sales as he talked his way into. His effectiveness as a salesman was weakened because he never gave the buyer a chance to tell *his* story. He was always talking, never listening. At sales meetings, he was always the first to raise his hand to ask questions. Actually, he just wanted to talk—to try impress the boss and his associates with how smart he was.

Despite many warnings and complaints from customers in his territory, Motor Mouth persisted in his continual talking. He was finally fired. He succeeded in talking his way out of a $21,000 a year job.

While most of us aren't the extreme case that Motor Mouth was, many of us often become so enthusiastic in getting an order that we are apt to get carried away with ourselves. I, myself, plead guilty to having spoken when I should have been listening.

Make Your Sale—Shut Up—Get Out

Although I had some excellent teachers early in my career as a salesman, the lessons that really stuck were the ones that I learned through my own blunders and stupidity. The story I am about to relate is one of these. It concerns a promotion on a new line of vinyl sheet goods. The patterns, six in number, were outstanding, the price was right, and the selling helps were among the best I had ever seen. In short—it was a natural! I had the undivided attention of one buyer for ten minutes and had given him one of my very best sales pitches. In fact, he picked out all six of the colors, and when I was writing up the order I was so pleased and enthused, I just kept on talking. I wanted him to be sure he knew how beautiful they were, and to impress upon him what a good buy he had made. While I was spouting off, he suddenly walked over to the samples I had laying on the floor, picked one up, and said, "I don't think I need all six colors. Leave out this one with the yellow in it and just send me a small roll of each of the other five." Well, that just about floored me and I wondered why he had changed his mind when he was so enthusiastic at first.

After I had finished writing the order, I thanked him for the business and was about to leave when I turned to him and asked, "I'm curious about something, Mr. Williams. Just why did you suddenly decide not to take the sixth color after you had initially selected it?"

"Very simple," he replied, looking at me like the cat who had just found out how to open the canary's cage, "you talked me out of it!"

While the loss of that roll of vinyl was a bitter pill for me to swallow, it was fortunate that it happened when I was starting out in the selling game. As a result, I established a **rule** that I followed for many years. It became such an important skill in my own selling arsenal that I am passing it along to you because it can mean money in your pocket. When you have made a sale, change the subject of conversation immediately. Write up the order as quickly as you can and leave before the buyer has a chance to change his mind. But above all, don't keep talking about your product! There is real power in those two little words—*shut up*. Keep them as a major weapon in your selling arsenal.

A well-known professor of Public Speaking at a large university closed his final lecture of the year to one of his classes by saying, "Now in summary, I want to give you a simple formula for a successful speech. It consists of three parts: (1) stand up, (2) speak up, (3) shut up. The first two parts are easy, but for reasons that I could never quite comprehend, it is the third part that most speakers find so difficult. When they get to that crucial point when they should sign off and sit down, they can't resist the temptation to keep on talking. It isn't long before they lose their audience. I have found that the best speeches are short speeches—those where the speaker knows when to shut up and sit down."

That professor could have given the same advice to a class in salesmanship or sales management. Knowing when to shut up is just as important to a salesperson as it is to a public speaker. The professor's formula for a good speech always works during a sales presentation to your buyer. It suggests another **rule** that every sales person should follow: (1) make your pitch, (2) make your sale, (3) make your exit.

Don't Let The "Social Hour" Kill Your Sale

The danger in "hanging around" after the sale has been made is that you may inadvertently say something that will cause the buyer to change his mind. Close the book, drop the subject of the sale, and get out! If you don't, you're asking for trouble.

Wes Blenton can give you a word of advice on this subject. He will tell you how he blew a nice order simply because he didn't pack up and leave the minute he had finished writing it up. He made the mistake of suggesting that he and the buyer have a cup of coffee. Wes had done an excellent job of selling the buyer a new line of bedroom furniture, and got an order for $4,000. Over coffee, the buyer started to ask questions and began to wonder if he had done the right thing in investing that much money in the new product. When, during the course of the conversation that ensued, the buyer learned that several other dealers in town would be buying some of the same line of merchandise, he began to cool off. Wes was put on the defensive, and tried to assure the buyer that his new product wouldn't be "footballed" by his competitors.

When Wes left the buyer he was concerned, but he still had the order in his pocket. That is, until he checked in with his office later in the day only to learn that the buyer had phoned in earlier and cancelled the entire order. $4,000 worth of business went down the drain because Wes didn't close up his order book and get out! That cup of coffee turned out to be expensive—it gave the buyer enough time to think about the order and re-open the entire subject. Had Wes packed up and left immediately, chances are good that the buyer would have forgetten about the purchase and turned his mind to other matters.

It is sometimes a very thin line between making the sale or losing it. Once you have buttoned it up, don't do anything that will give the buyer a chance or an excuse to change his mind. That is his prerogative, of course, but just the *sight* of you can make him think of reasons why he shouldn't have bought your product. After the sale, clear out just as quickly as you can!

Wes would agree with the rule to: (1) stand up, (2) speak up, and (3) shut up, but he would also add, "then get out of there before something happens to turn your buyer off." Wes learned the hard way, as have so many salespersons, that a written order is nothing more than a piece of scrap paper, until the merchandise is shipped.

HOW TO USE YOUR EARS TO TALK YOUR WAY TO SUCCESSFUL SALES

It is a common misconception that silence and listening are negative factors—the first the absence of sound, the second the absence of talking. I have a contrary opinion. I strongly believe that they are both positive forces, and that a capacity for silence and listening is just as important to the salesperson as his ability to talk.

Always bear in mind that a sales presentation is not a monologue. It is a verbal sparring match in which both the salesperson and the buyer participate. It is a word contest that can never end in a tie. There is always a winner and a loser—the salesperson either makes the sale or loses it; the buyer either buys or doesn't buy. Whichever way it goes, the end result usually depends on the effectiveness of the salesperson's presentation—how well he has talked, and also how well he has listened his way to the sale.

You have to be able to use all the skills and techniques that are available to you, along with a lot of moxie and know-how, if you expect to make it in the selling game. That's what this book is all about. However, you'll never achieve your objective—getting the order—without doing some listening somewhere along the line.

Win Oldham, an electric kitchen equipment salesman, was once asked what he attributed his success to. He was quick to reply, "I always come in on my buyer and try to throw out a couple of thoughts to get him talking. Pretty soon he is making my pitch for me. All I do is sit back and listen and answer questions. Makes him feel real smart and important. The thing is—everybody loves to talk. That's the trouble with most salesmen. They yak, yak, yak, and all the time the buyer is trying to get *his* word in. In this business you've got to keep your ears open and listen. You've got to find out what your buyer's thinking, which you can't do when your mouth's flapping. When you let him talk and spill it out, then you know what you have to do to knock over the order."

Listening seemed to work well for Oldham. He listened his way to $29,000 a year.

I was recently given a new definition of a bore. You ask someone how he feels and he proceeds to tell you. That's not too far from the truth, because it is a well-known fact that most people, given the opportunity, will talk about themselves. The same holds true with reference to almost any subject. They usually don't care what the other fellow thinks—"just let *me* talk!"

Regardless of how well prepared you are in product knowledge and how much know-how you have, things don't always go the way you planned. You have to be prepared for having the buyer butt in on your presentation at any time, sometimes bringing up something that has nothing to do with the subject under consideration. When that happens to you, you have to stop pulling in on your selling reel and let out line—let your buyer talk while you listen. Hear him out, because in talking, he will give you information that will be useful to you so you will know when to start reeling in again.

HOW TO USE YOUR EYES TO TALK YOUR WAY TO SUCCESSFUL SALES

One salesman once said that selling is a cat and mouse game between the salesperson and the buyer. That is probably true, but I am sure there have been times when you have wondered which was the mouse!

Assuming that the salesperson is the pursuer, I think a lesson can be learned from the manner in which the cat stalks a mouse. It doesn't rush in blindly—it gives it the soft sell instead of the hard sell. It lies there, outwardly unconcerned, licking its paws, while watching and waiting. Only the flick of its tail belies its apparently calm demeanor. When its eyes tell it that the mouse is about to get away, it makes a quick move and springs on it.

Facial Expressions Can Be Meaningful

You must not only listen to the buyer, but you have to watch him during your presentation. Have the patience of the cat! Changes in facial expression can be very meaningful to you—they could well provide you with a clue as to what he is thinking. You can usually tell by watching your buyer's eyes, if you are "coming through" to him.

In Chapter 3 I told about Frank Sissonne, the ex-sales clerk, ex-bank teller, who became president of a small mid-western bank. Sissonne made it because of his simplicity, but also because he was an artful watcher and listener. I was told that he would sit for moments on end, stroking his chin and leaning back in his old leather chair, watching and listening, using his ears and eyes to get his client's reactions. He literally "stalked" his client, waiting for the exact moment to go in for the kill.

On the social circuit, a good conversationalist is someone who watches and listens, and says little. The same can be applied to good salesmanship. Executive suites and brass rows of many companies are inhabited by former salespersons who were good watchers and listeners on their way up. One of these was Irv Lacey, salesman for a furniture manufacturer. The president of one of his large distributors told Lacey's boss one day, "You've got a good man in that Lacey. I enjoy having him in my office and talking with him. He just sits there and sort of glares and listens while I spill out what's on my mind. He never has much to say, but when he does talk, believe me, you pay attention. He's got the darndest eyes—he doesn't look at you, he looks through you. Everyone likes him. No wonder he is such a good salesman. He'll make a great sales manager some day!"

Although Irv Lacey was doing quite well financially as a manufacturer's salesman, he subsequently was hired by the distributor as sales manager at a 40% increase in salary. Lacey had know-how and used the skills and techniques of selling, but it was his ability to know when to watch and listen and keep his mouth buttoned up, that made him a standout. It paid off for him as it can for you.

Use Your Eyes To Detect Stock Changes

A smart salesperson uses his eyes not only to observe the reactions of the buyer, but in a more specific way, to determine the merchandise needs of his customer. He develops a photographic eye that tells him from one call to the next what changes have taken place in the dealer's stock—what has sold out, any competitive products that have moved in, etc. Every good salesperson knows what his best sellers are, and when he walks on a display floor, the first thing he looks for is to see if any of them are missing. His eyes tell him what to zero in on. If you don't have your best sellers showing on the dealer's floor, you are losing business.

Ideally, the one ambition of all salespersons is to build up a coterie of loyal accounts. You'll never be able to achieve this 100% but you can certainly try. Jimmy Winters, one of our salesmen, once defined a loyal customer as "one you keep so loaded and stacked up with your own merchandise that he can't afford to buy from anyone else." There is a lot of truth in this. Simply stated, if *you* don't sell the buyer and keep him loaded, someone else will. And the more "holes" you leave in his stock, the better the chances of your competition moving in on you. Use your eyes to guard your position—don't lose business by default.

Jimmy was quicker with his eyes and hands than any other salesman I ever worked with. He would size up a stock inventory and in five minutes could tell what had been sold and how much yardage was in each roll of the remaining patterns. When he confronted his buyer, he knew exactly what he was going to sell him.

Jimmy once said, "You have to be a bit 'nosey' to make it in this business. Get all the information you can before you start in on the buyer. Your eyes can tell you a lot about what he needs. I never go into a buyer's office without first making a quick survey of his stock."

It paid off for Jimmy. His advancements were frequent and he became a star performer as a salesman before subsequently moving up into management.

HOW TO USE THE QUESTION AND ANSWER TECHNIQUE TO TALK YOUR WAY TO SALES

This is a technique that is often used by experienced salespersons—sometimes known as the *Socratic Method*. *Webster's New World Dictionary*, Second College Edition, defines the Socratic Method: "the dialectical method of teaching or discussion used by Socrates, involving the asking of a series of questions that inevitably lead the answerer to a logical conclusion foreseen by the questioner."

For the purposes of salesmanship, the Socratic Method is the technique of getting the buyer into the act by asking him a question or questions, then listening to find out what he is thinking, and then helping him sell himself on your product.

It is a three-way system: (1) ask (2) listen, and (3) focus.

This method has long been effectively used by many experienced salespersons. First, you ask the prospective customer what he thinks about your product. Naturally, he is anxious to talk, so while he talks, you listen. You listen for him to tell you something. You take your cue and then start telling him what he wants to hear by focusing on something he has told you. It is significant that you can make the Socratic technique work only if you have the capacity to listen. Getting him to talk is the easy part—it's the listening on your part that is often so difficult.

Zed Binkley, an automobile salesman, was an expert in the use of the Socratic Method. I once went to an automobile show floor with my wife to look at new year models which had just been announced. She wanted to trade in her then current model on a new one. I went along, but made a secret pledge to myself that I wouldn't butt in. She would have to make her own decision!

We were standing, admiring a very attractive two-door model, when Zed Binkley came up to us and introduced himself. He had already seen the look of admiration on my wife's face, so he turned to her while he patted the hood of the car, and asked, "Don't you think it's a beautiful car?"

My wife responded, "Yes, it's extremely nice looking."

Binkley pursued his questioning; "Tell me, what do you like the most about the car?"

She replied, "I love the contrast between the azure color and the white vinyl top. And those wire wheels give it such an elegant look."

Binkley went on, "Would you like to try sitting behind the wheel?"

When my wife said she would, he opened the door, she got in and remarked, "My, how comfortable—and the light blue upholstery goes so well with the exterior."

Binkley went on,"Are you pleased with the performance of your present car?"

She replied, "Well—yes, but I think the mileage . . . "

Binkley interrupted her, saying, "Suppose I were to tell you that the gas comsumption on the new model is 20% less than on your car?"

She quickly replied, "Oh, I would love that!"

Space does not permit me to relate the entire conversation between Binkley and my wife, but by asking her questions, he learned three things: (1) she liked the color, the vinyl top, and the wire wheels; (2) she liked the interior comfort of the car; and (3) she was interested in economy of performance. Armed with this information, Binkley went to work focusing on them. First he used the ego appeal technique, telling her how elegant the car was. (Yes, he even used the exact word my wife did!) He told her how proud she would be to drive it. He talked about the comfort and beauty of the interior of the car. He then switched over to the practical appeal technique by pointing out in simple terms changes that had been made to make for better performance and better mileage.

Zed Binkley proceeded to sell my wife that car by "setting her up," by using the question and answer technique. I stood by, listening and admiring the manner in which he used his selling skills—even though it cost me money! The result: he made a $14,500 sale.

Salespersons at the wholesaler-retailer level can also put the Socratic Method to good use. Since the buyer has to be convinced that your product will be profitable for him, what better way is there than to let him convince himself! Let him talk your way to an order by answering your questions. Many salesperson inadvertently use the Socratic Method and don't realize how powerful a selling technique it is. If you deliberately set out to use the question and answer technique you will soon discover that it can be one of your most effective selling skills.

Ellis Carlton was a factory representative who mastered the use of this technique. Ellis was known as a "knickknack" salesman. He handled many imported items, from watches and electronic equipment, to sweaters, shirts, and other sundry wearing apparel. He said he would handle anything where he "could make a buck." Ellis always followed a two-pronged procedure: (1) he carried in samples of only one line on his calls on a given day, and (2) he rehearsed in advance just how he would display his samples and present that line.

He would always start out by laying his samples on the desk of his buyer, and before he said a word about his product asked, "How do these grab you?", or "What do you like the most about these?" Sometimes, of course, he got a negative answer, such as "They're for the birds," or "You couldn't give them to me." For the most part, however, the buyer would answer more directly while Ellis listened for some clue, some word, to build his pitch around. Key words, such as "They're *unusual* or *different*;" or "They look *sharp* or *cheap*;" or "They look *shabby or sturdy*;" or "They are too *large* or too *small*." Just one little word—that's all Ellis was looking for. Once he heard it, whether it was disapproval or approbation, he knew what the buyer was thinking and therefore knew what direction to take in his sales pitch. One word—it told him much. Using this technique worked well for Ellis Carlton. He asked and listened his way to $26,000 a year.

Use the Socratic Method to bring out what the buyer likes about your product—and also what he doesn't like about it. Either way, you have tested his mind and by getting him to talk, you get him into your act. Once you establish a basis—knowing what he is thinking—then you can swing into the other selling techniques that are available to you. Ask and then listen. It has worked for others and will work for you.

8

HOW TO TURN COMPLAINTS AND PROBLEMS INTO SALES

No doubt you have said many times to yourself, "If it wasn't for problems and complaints, this would be a pretty good business." Perhaps you are right, but one thing you can always count on. As long as you are doing business, you will have problems and complaints; and the more you sell, the more you will be faced with. How you handle them can well determine what kind of salesperson you are. One word of advice. Take care of your own problems and complaints and don't try to fluff them off on your boss or somebody else. It won't work.

This is a subject that most writers seem to carefully avoid, but I believe it is a very important part of selling, so I am tackling it head-on. I can't think of a single area that causes salespersons more frustrations and headaches. Nothing will shake up the average salesperson more than being greeted by the buyer with those fateful words, "I have a complaint," or "I have a problem." What happens when a buyer greets you with this bombshell? Do you back away and try to brush it off, or do you face up to him, take the situation by the hand, and say, "I'm sorry to hear that. What can I do to help you get it squared away?"

Too much emphasis is placed on the distasteful aspects of complaints and problems, whereas in fact, they can be used to produce beneficial results. Problems and complaints are like diseases—they can only be cured by prompt and proper treatment. If expeditiously handled, they can even give you beneficial side effects. For example, during World War II when doctors were treating malaria patients, they learned that quinine has a tendency to stabilize the heart beat and control fibrillations. The outcome was the development of quinidine, now a widely used drug. These positive results were attained because doctors recognized definite side benefits in the treatment of a severe disease. You can do the same in the matter of handling complaints and problems.

In this business of selling you have to be a salesperson, a teacher, a counselor, a trouble shooter, and a diplomat, among other things. You are always in the middle: on the one hand, an object of the wants and unfair demands of your customers; and on the other, a ready target for the requests and pressures of over-anxious sales managers. In the matter of dealing with problems and complaints, there are a number of basic **rules** that can help you to effectively handle this important aspect of your business:

1. Never let personalities enter into a complaint or problem. Always maintain an impersonal posture at all times.
2. Don't ever get trapped by any thoughts that complaints will "go away" by themselves. They only grow, and with time become more complex and intense.
3. Always prepare for the worst—but expect the best.
4. Face up to every situation squarely and unafraid, but don't ever start anything you can't finish.

5. Hear out the other person. Remember, there are always two sides to everything. Don't try to hush him up. Encourage him to keep talking and get things off his chest. Remember the importance of being a good listener.
6. Never argue. Keep your voice low, and above all, don't lose your cool.
7. Carefully assemble and consider the facts of the situation—then act accordingly.
8. Try, if possible, to find the humorous side of every situation. People can't laugh and be mad at the same time.
9. Encourage your customers to bring their complaints to you, and not to your competitiors.
10. Be willing to take the rap if you or your company makes a mistake.

Add these rules to your arsenal of selling skills. They can help you over some of the rough spots in settling complaints and problems.

HOW TO MAKE THE MOST OF LEGITIMATE PRODUCT COMPLAINTS

If your customer has a legitimate complaint concerning your product, you should be the first to want to know about it. Don't be surprised when complaints arise, because the law of averages dictates that things will go wrong from time to time in any manufacturing process. I have learned from experience that even though the complaint may seem to be a small thing to you, it is usually magnified in the eyes of your customer. It therefore becomes imperative that when he registers a complaint with you, get right on top of it! Stay with it until it is drawn to a satisfactory conclusion.

Settle Justified Complaints Without Hesitation!

In every business it can be anticipated that a certain percentage of dollar sales will go down the drain because of credit losses. It's just a part of doing business! The same is true of money spent on the settlement of complaints. It is to be expected and should be no cause for alarm! There is one basic **rule** that must always be followed, however. If a complaint is justified, get it settled quickly and without any hesitation. Trying to waltz around such a complaint by procrastination only creates hard feelings and frustrations. Many people have a chip on their shoulder when they find that something has gone wrong with your product, and your failure to take immediate action will leave you with a situation of "everything lost and nothing gained." When you know you are going to have to spend money on a complaint, get it done right now so you will derive some positive benefit from it. Get your money's worth if you can!

One benefit that should always result from the prompt settlement of a product complaint is the reassurance you give your customer that in dealing with you he has a source of supply that is reliable and stands behind its products. Make it a point to tell him this on every complaint you settle for him. If you have to pay out $100 on a claim, be sure that you get $100 worth of good will for it! There is no area where the technique of dependency is more effective than in the settling of complaints. If he knows you are reliable and that he can count on you to take care of your product problems, he will want to do business with you.

What kind of a reputation do you have with your customers? Are you a quibbler, afraid to face up to a situation? Are your customers wary of you because you dillydally and have difficulty in making decisions and then standing on them? Or do you grab the complaint by the neck and shake it down before it can get away from you?

Profit By Quick Handling Of Legitimate Complaints

Proper handling of legitimate complaints can also result in direct additional business for you. A classical example is the case of Ned Summers, one of our salesmen, who was asked by a dealer to inspect a linoleum floor installed in the kitchen at the Borst residence. When Ned saw the floor, he quickly discovered that the material was defective, and just as quickly so advised Mrs. Borst, telling her it would be replaced at her convenience—at no cost to her. She had prepared herself for an argument, and was so surprised and impressed by Ned's quick action that she couldn't wait to tell her husband that night. He was a prominent doctor who headed up a medical group that was constructing a new building. His architect had specified another brand of flooring material, but as a result of the manner in which Mrs. Borst's complaint was handled, he insisted that our product be installed. As he said in explanation to his colleagues, "They stand behind their products."

There was no question about that floor in the Borst's kitchen. It was defective material and had to be replaced. By acting promptly, Ned turned the complaint into a good contract job that increased his dollar volume almost $8,000.

Failure to accept responsibility for defects in your product can result in loss of business for you. For the most part, your buyers know almost as much about your products as you do, so they can recognize defects when they see them. Don't underestimate their intelligence! One legitimate complaint, improperly handled, can set up a chain reaction that can be disastrous for you. Failure to back up a warranty on your products will not only generate hard feelings, but can result in the loss of business—even the loss of a customer.

HOW TO HANDLE NON-LEGITIMATE PRODUCT COMPLAINTS

When you get into the area of non-legitimate complaints, you are moving into quicksand and it therefore becomes necessary for you to exercise great care. You know there is nothing wrong with your product, but your customer, and perhaps his customer, persist in thinking otherwise. Speed in expediting the settlement of this type of complaint is extremely important because emotions usually get involved, often at a "sickly" level. The more emotional a situation becomes, the more difficult it is for you to handle.

Many take the position that regardless of circumstances, the customer is always right. I totally disagree, and sumbit a contrary opinion. The customer definitely isn't always right! In fact, the customer can at times be so wrong that his complaints smell of pure subterfuge, and as far as I am concerned, should definitely be treated as such. You are going to run into such situations every day. The question is, how do you handle them?

People who persist in pursuing non-legitimate complaints usually fall in three general classifications:

1. The lowest form is the one who deliberately sets out to "take" others for all they can get.
2. There are the chronic complainers—those who look at everything through a magnifying glass. These have usually been "taken" at one time by some unscrupulous person, so they have their guard up.
3. Then there are those who sincerely feel that the product does not meet up with their expectations—even though they often admit that they abused it.

Those Who Deliberately Set Out To "Take" Others For All They Can Get

In this group you will find the discount hounds, the free loaders, the "get something for nothing" freaks, who are fast-growing cancers in the marketplace. If something goes wrong, regardless of who is at fault, they cry out, "Stick the manufacturers—they're big and can afford it. Let the insurance people pick up the tab—they're loaded with money."

Several years ago I had the occasion to lock horns with one of those discount buffs—a Mr. Sandner. He had built a four story office building in which one of our flooring contractors had installed a sizeable quantity of our flooring materials. Sandner soon complained to the dealer that the floor was defective because he contended it was difficult to keep clean. He demanded a substantial discount on the cost of the floors. When the dealer told him the problem was in the maintenance techniques he was using and refused to make any kind of cash settlement with Sandner, he demanded that the manufacturer's representative inspect the floor. At that point, I entered the scene and confirmed the finding of our dealer. Then Sandner really got out his ugly pills. He made threats (a typical pattern for this kind of person). "I'll write to your president, I'll get your job," etc., etc.

How do you handle that kind of a situation? You take a firm approach. I pulled out one of my calling cards, wrote our president's name and address on the reverse side, handed it to Sandner, and said, "Be my guest." I then walked out amidst a vocal barrage of nasty diatribes. As I predicted, he did write to our president, completely misrepresenting the facts, (another characteristic of this type of person). When I explained the truth of the matter to our president, he wrote to Sandner telling him he could find no fault with my findings and decision and that our company, therefore, considered the matter a closed issue.

I heard later from others that Sandner had "discounted" the cost of his building and everything else he bought by 20% by making false claims against every subcontractor on the job. Many gave in, just to get him off their back. He was ruthless. Taking a firm stand paid off for me in that I gained the respect of my dealer, who was pleased that "you didn't knuckle down to that dirty s.o.b." Because of this complaint, the dealer and I established a rapport that paid off well for me in increased business in the years to come. Besides, Sandner kept on berating me and my company for several years, and I am sure that his knocks produced a lot of good business for us.

The Chronic Complainers—Those Who Look At Everything Through A Magnifying Glass

These are the perfectionists who always take a close look at any new product they purchase. They buy a new refrigerator and immediately start to look for small nicks and chips in the enamel. These people are not usually vicious, as was the case with Sandner. All they want is to get their "money's worth." "I didn't buy seconds. When I pay for perfect merchandise, I expect to get perfect merchandise." How do you deal with this kind of customer?

Martin Branner, a top refrigerator salesman, once said, "First and foremost, make certain that lines of communication are always kept open with them. The best approach is to agree with them—that the little nick does detract from the beauty of the machine, but how fortunate it is that synthetic paints are available so that an expert can cover it so it would never be noticed. I always tell the customer, 'It's no problem at all. We'll have our man out this afternoon or tomorrow morning, whichever is more convenient for you. Meanwhile, you go over your refrigerator carefully so he will be sure to catch all other small blemishes.'

"Lean over backward with these people to make certain they know you are there to help them and that you are not there to talk you way out of a complaint. Let them know it is seldom that a manufacturer can turn out a product that is completely perfect. The salesperson has to bear that in mind and try to convey it to the purchaser. Properly done, without hesitation or haggling as to who might be responsible, chances are excellent that the customer will understand and that the necessary small repairs will rectify the situation. It may cost a few dollars, but you end up with a satisfied customer."

Because of his expertise in handling complaints Branner each year won a bonus of $1,500 because he kept his claim payments below a percentage of sale figures established annually by his company. His know-how paid off well for him.

One Difficult Type Of Complaint Is Where There Is Nothing Wrong With The Product, But The Customer Has Abused It.

A product can perform in accordance with its warranties, but due to no fault of the manufacturer, something happens so the customer becomes unhappy. Sometimes there are borderline cases, but for the most part the customer is to blame. Being able to identify with the customer—putting yourself in his place—is extremely important.

Always look for a way to compromise on a complaint. Even though you *know that the customer is wrong and the complaint is not justified, every effort should be made to work out some kind of a compromise. Always think in terms of keeping the customer—they are hard to get and so easy to lose.*

The use of *policy settlements* can be a very effective selling tool in the adjudication of complaints. Sure it costs money to make settlements of this nature, but if you keep a customer happy, you will get future business that will more than pay for the amount you put out.

Anyone who was ever in the carpet business can tell you that staining complaints are the toughest kind to handle, because chances are good that the problem stems from abuse rather than from any inherent weakness in the material itself. But try to tell that to the customer!

Dick DiBeatro told about a complaint he was on—a Mrs. Claye, whose poodle had urinated in the center of a room of costly white carpet, leaving a stain. "Mrs. Claye, with much righteous indignation, stated that the little mistake her darling little Pierre made could not possibly have resulted in such an awful spot on her new $50.00 a yard carpet. The material just *had* to be defective—that's all there was to it!

"What do you do? Your dealer is in a bind because Mrs. Claye is an old customer and throughout the years has purchased thousands of dollars of merchandise from him, so he can't afford to lose her any more than you can afford to lose him! The answer is to find some way to compromise. You agree with her that the spot made by Pierre is unsightly, but at the same time try to tell her that these things happen every day and fortunately there is a happy solution to the problem. Mrs. Claye must be assured in no uncertain terms that there is nothing wrong with her carpet, and that there isn't a carpet made that will withstand mistakes made by pets. I had to let her know that even though we as the manufacturer are not responsible, we do want to help eliminate the unsightly spot where Pierre did his business. I always feel we should take credit for being cooperative! Through modern installation techniques, our craftsmen can cut out the stained spot in the floor and insert a new piece so expertly, that it would be impossible for the customer to see where the work was done.

"By spending a few dollars on a policy settlement I made Mrs. Claye happy and also made my dealer happy. How much better for everyone than had I taken the position, 'The dog did it. There is absolutely nothing we can do for you. It is not our responsibility!' I find that a little patience and understanding works most of the time. I think spending 25 bucks to save a $1,900 job of carpet is good business, even though we are not at fault. That 25 dollars will come back to us some day."

Of course, when you bump into an unreasonable individual who refuses to let your craftsman put in a small patch, your position would have to be, "It's not our fault, but even so we are willing to pay for a small spot replacement. From our point of view there isn't anything further that can be done. I suggest that you accept our offer of good will."

If the customer persists in demanding a complete free replacement, or insists on a large cash settlement—my answer is to suggest to her that she discuss her problem with Mr. Sandner.

Be Courageous In Handling Complaints

For some reason, many people feel that whenever they register a complaint of any kind, they are automatically entitled to some kind of an adjustment. It would be easy for a manufacturer's representative to bow down to every wish of every customer, but along with an obligation to be fair to the customer is his responsibility to be fair to his own company. Complaint settlements can be costly, and if you are indiscriminate in the manner in which you spend money on them, you will soon find yourself eating into your own profits.

It is difficult to take a position that the customer doesn't agree with, because personal abuse will without question come into the picture. You just have to harden your shell and if you know that what you are doing is fair to the customer and also to the company you represent, you're going to have to eat crow. When you do, eat it with dignity! Once you become weak and permit others to browbeat you through threats and abuse, you are finished.

Always remember—when you are faced with a complaint, you are put in a defensive position. Take it in stride. If the complaint is justified, settle it quickly. If it is a borderline case, try to compromise with a policy statement. If someone is out to "take" you and your company, have no part of them. Tell them "NO" and stand by your guns. And finally, even though the customer is completely wrong and has abused your product, try to work out a compromise of some kind to keep everyone happy. If they refuse, *then* it's time for you to hang tough.

I always followed a **rule**: just because someone is complaining to you gives them no right to rub your nose in the dirt, so don't ever let that happen to you. Stand tall. Don't ever let a complaint of any nature lower your dignity!

HOW TO EFFECTIVELY HANDLE ERRORS IN SHIPPING AND BILLING

When you walk into a situation where you face an irate customer because of an error made in your shipping or billing departments—tread cautiously. Such errors usually involve loss of money, so your customer will inevitably be emotionally upset. Mistakes are bound to happen, but the better prepared you are to cope with them the sooner you will get your customer calmed down.

There are a number of basic **rules** you must always follow when you run into problems of this kind:

1. Never try to make light of the situation. Problems and errors are not a laughing matter and when they occur, it's definitely not the time to bring in the whistles and funny hats.
2. Always keep cool. If your customer becomes unreasonable and says uncomplimentary things about you, your product, or your company—just stay calm and listen. Let the customer blow off steam, but don't let yourself get involved in any arguments. When he's mad, he's itching for a good fight, so silence is your only line of defense.
3. Always maintain a sympathetic attitude toward your customer. When he gets all steamed up because of an error, use the agreement technique. Just a few statements like the following can work wonders for you:
   a. "I don't blame you one bit for feeling as you do Mr. Smith. I would personally be just as mad."
   b. "There's simply no excuse for it to have happened. I would be just as upset as you."
   c. "I'm going to get at the bottom of this thing right away. I give you my word—I'll get it all straightened out."
   d. "Now don't you worry about this one bit more. Just leave it for me to handle. This thing is ridiculous!"
4. Try not to get involved in credit matters. Sales and credit are two separate functions. Any matters pertaining to credit should be referred to your credit department.
5. Always put the buyer at ease by being patient with him. Here again, being a good listener is one of the best tools in your arsenal.
6. Never run down your company. Don't agree with your customer if he should tell you that you are working for a lousy outfit. Just remind him that you will see to it that the error is rectified, but never downgrade your own company just because an error has occurred.

7. Don't try to pass the buck to someone else in your company. It is *your* customer, and it is up to you to get matters resolved.
8. Exercise speed in correcting errors. The longer a problem remains unsolved, the harder it will be to get squared away.

How To Handle Mistakes

No two cases are alike, but regardless of what has happened, the use of good old common sense will go a long way toward solving most problems. Basically, there are only two things that can be done when there has been an error in shipment:

1. Suggest that the merchandise shipped in error be returned immediately, at no cost to the customer. This is the easy way out and sometimes it is the only way to settle with a customer who is hot under the collar.
2. Use the compromise method whenever possible. This involves the customer keeping the merchandise, either at some kind of an extra discount, or an extension of payment time to enable him to move it without being penalized.

Discuss these alternatives with your customer and then let *him* make the decision. When he decides, then the monkey is off your back.

SOME HELPFUL TIPS TO TURN PROBLEMS INTO POSITIVE RESULTS

One thing is certain about problems, and that is that all customers react differently towards them. The least little matter will upset some to the point where they push the panic button, while there are dealers who use problems to throw salespersons off the track and divert them from their job of trying to sell. It would be extremely difficult to make a general categorization of all problems and the manner in which customers react to them, but there are a few general skills that can always be helpful.

Some Buyers Are Professional Moaners

Nothing is ever right with them. They dote on chewing out the salesperson over the least little thing. They can either make your life miserable or they can give you a rare opportunity to practice the art of listening. Usually this type wants to talk. He knows the cure-alls for all of the ills of the world, but when it comes to his own business affairs he is full of feelings of insecurity. As a result, something is always bugging him and the only way to handle him is to let him talk and get things off his chest. Then and only then—after he has let the gas out of his own balloon—can you settle down to the business of trying to sell him.

Encourage Your Customers To Come To You With Their Problems

Earlier in the book we discussed the use of the technique of dependency and at this point emphasize the importance of its use in the matter of handling problems. Most buyers are "loners" and are aching to have someone to talk things over with. Making decisions is one of the most difficult things most people are confronted with, and your customer is no exception. He is going to find someone he can confide in—if it isn't you, it may well be one of your competitors. Don't ever get yourself locked up in that kind of a situation! If you are fulfilling your responsibility of being his counselor, then he will always feel free to come to you for your opinion on matters pertaining to his business. Sometimes he will get himself in a financial bind and will ask you for an opinion as to what to do. It is at such times that your knowledge of his business, along with a general know-how, can be extremely helpful. One word of advice in the matter of trying to counsel with him on his problems: *don't get mixed up in his personal problems*. Otherwise, you might be inviting disaster.

Don't Try To Dodge Problems Because They Are Unpleasant And Burdensome

We all worry about problems, and the stickier they are, the more we would like to brush them aside and go on to more pleasant things. Unfortunately, it just doesn't work that way. Those problems are a part of your business, and the more you procrastinate in getting them solved, the more they are going to snowball on you until ultimately a point is reached where you can't handle them.

Try to make each problem a challenge. There is always an answer to every situation, good or bad. You will soon learn that the more effective you are at solving problems, the better a salesperson you will become. Proper handling of complaints and problems always has been the mark of a good salesperson.

Handle Your Problems Personally

When your customer tells you he has a problem concerning your products or your company, the very worst thing you can do is tell him, "I'll pass it along. You'll be hearing from my people." Wouldn't it be wonderful if you could brush off your problems just like that? I can tell you from the experiences of many salespersons, however, that it won't work! As far as your customer is concerned, *you* are the company, and he expects you to wash any linen that has become dirty because of some mistake. When you are handling an account, you handle it all—the orders as well as the complaints and problems. You're going to have to take the bitter with the sweet! It's impossible for you or anyone else to have all of the answers, but never hesitate to use those powerful words, "Give me time, and I'll find out!" How much more effective is this approach than to simply admit defeat and turn the problem over to somebody else! You will gain the respect of your customer and a desire on his part to cooperate with you. This alone will help to expedite the settlement of any problem. Always remember he is your customer and his problems therefore become your problems. Treat them as such and you will experience success in problem handling.

Unfortunately, many salespersons are not capable of handling their problems and complaints. Louie Poster, sales representative for a line of hardware sundries, did well in selling, but was a failure in handling problems. Somehow he just couldn't get it through his head that problems were his responsibility—he persisted in trying to find someone else to lean on whenever he was faced with one. He usually went crying to his boss or others in his sales organization. Needless to say, they all had their own share of problems and resented Louie trying to unload his problems on them.

His boss, Bob Davis, was patient and understanding and did all he could to straighten Louie out. He used a procedure that has worked well in most cases. It is a **rule** that I recommend to all sales managers: Don't let your salespersons lay their problems on your desk. Tell them, instead, that you will always be available to discuss their own proposed solutions to their problems. This procedure forces the salesperson to try to reach his own conclusions. Davis tried this on Louie, but he just wasn't able to cut it. He seemed to come unhinged every time a problem or complaint faced him, and he became so flustered he couldn't make decisions on his own. After a long period of sweating it out with Louie, Davis finally had to let him go.

Louie Poster lost a job that paid him $24,000 a year because he wasn't a complete salesman. Louie could sell—but that was all. You can learn a lesson from Louie. If you are weak in the complaint and problems aspect of your work, now is the time to shore up your capabilities. It isn't easy, but it can be done. I have seen other salespersons completely change their lives by adopting a healthy new approach to handling the problems and complaints in their business.

9

HOW TO PLAN YOUR WORK AND WORK YOUR PLAN

Can you conceive of a team of physicians and surgeons going into an operating room for open heart surgery without having each step carefully planned, so that every surgeon and nurse knows exactly what his or her part of the overall effort will be? Have you experienced the boredom of listening to a speaker—a politician or even a minister—who hasn't carefully prepared for his presentation; or if he has, meanders from the central theme of his plan? And of course, there are the so-called salespersons who obviously haven't given any serious thought to planning their work and working their plans. I resent very much the name "huckster" or "peddler" being put on anyone in our profession, but if a salesperson is guilty of not planning his work and stumbles along haphazardly, he deserves such a title.

I have never met a top salesperson who did not assiduously plan his work. I refer to the stars in the profession, regardless of what their product is. You better take inventory and make sure that you are a good planner yourself, if you have aspirations of being a successful salesperson in your own chosen field. If you are not a good organizer—if you don't plan your work and work your plan—I can assure you that you are going to have a rough time trying to talk your way to successful selling.

HOW CAREFUL PLANNING CAN PRODUCE SUCCESSFUL SALES

Good planning is as essential to good selling as are product knowledge and know-how. It is through planning, both long term and short term, that you determine in advance what course of action you will take to be effective in helping you talk your way to successful selling. Planning is the process of putting things together—organizing your selling skills and establishing timetables for implementing the use of the tools in your selling arsenal.

How To Use Long Term Goals To Talk Your Way To Successful Selling

Just as every business must each year establish budgets for expenditures, and project sales for the twelve month period ahead, so must you, the salesperson, set your own long term goals. Jonas Salk would have never developed his vaccine to prevent poliomyelitis, and Madam Curie would have never discovered polonium and radium, if they hadn't established long term goals.

There used to be an old cliché that told us not to try to shoot for the moon. NASA and the astronauts obviously didn't pay attention to it. They not only shot for the moon, but they actually put men on it—a feat that never could have been accomplished without long range planning. Salk, Curie, NASA, and many others set goals that were difficult, to be sure, but they knew that they were not dealing with the impossible—so they achieved their objectives.

When you make your own long term plans, be sure you are being practical and realistic. Don't reach out for the impossible, but fix goals for yourself that will enable you to talk your way to increased sales with full confidence. There are a number of things you have to consider when you make your long term plans.

Set your dollar volume goal for the year ahead. Ask yourself at the beginning of each year how much business you expect to do during the ensuing period. Budget your sales on a monthly basis, so as the year develops you will know exactly how you are progressing. If you are working for a corporation, no doubt your sales budget will be established by your sales management.

In this connection, I would like to inject a word of advice to management. Always be reasonable in what you expect of your salespersons. Don't let yourself get carried away with any thoughts of "mission impossible"—expecting your people to achieve unfair and unattainable goals. I suggest that when sales quotas are established, you base them on what you, yourself, could accomplish. It is indeed frustrating for a salesperson to be given a quota when he knows full well that it is impossible for him to reach it. When a salesperson is put in that kind of a pressure cooker, his work is no longer a challenge to him and he will lose his effectiveness. On the other hand, if quotas are set up that are fair and reasonable, your salespersons will make money for you as well as for themselves, and that's always the bottom line.

Good budgeting of dollar volume takes on a special significance when salespersons are paid a bonus based on their performance against quota. I once knew a hospital supply salesman named Jake Teiler who annually made a bonus of 20% to 30% of his base pay. Early each year Jake sat down with his management to arrive at a figure for his projected dollar sales for that year. Achieving 100%

of that quota gave him an automatic 10% bonus on his pay. Above that, based on a sliding scale of performance against quota, Jake could earn as much as a 50% bonus. Jake always did well, even when it seemed his quota was a tough one. Due to the bonus incentive program, which gave him an opportunity to make money, he stepped up his efforts and always ended up in a high bracket. Teiler was living proof of the fact that if you give a salesperson a fair objective, he will always come through.

Establish specific targets for the year ahead. Which of your prospective customers that you are presently not selling, but whose business you really want and need, are the ones you will concentrate on during the year? Single them out for your long range plans and then get together your tools in your selling arsenal and set up programs to zero in on them. Consider each a challenge for the year and keep an up-to-date record on your progress.

In the seat next to me on a jetliner sat a young man named Tip Scanlon who told me he was a partner in a small advertising agency in a metropolitan area. We spoke of many things, but I was particularly interested in his comments concerning the necessity for establishing specific targets in making long range plans. His specialty was trademark designs and marketing programs. He carried a beautifully designed brochure in his briefcase containing complete information on ten major "targets" he had set up for himself.

Scanlon told me, "A lot of companies spend a lot of wasted money each year on advertising. Today the potential for waste is greater than it ever has been because of the unbelievable barrage of over 1,000 messages a day that are beamed at each of us. Unless the reader or viewer knows whose message it is, the money spent is going down a rat hole. I try to get my prospective clients interested in building an *image*—one that everybody will recognize immediately. That's what I'm trying to sell these prospects," he concluded, as he patted the brochure in his hand.

When we left the plane, I told him that I would be very much interested in receiving word from him as to how he made out. I heard from him several months later and learned that he had sold two of his prospects. One was a corporation for which he designed a total graphic system including letterheads, insignias, truck decals, and identification for all other equipment and services—all bearing a new company trademark. Because he established long term goals, it was possible for this enterprising young salesman in a highly competitive field to talk his way to some very worthwhile business. I have no way of knowing the financial details of his transaction, but it was quite apparent that this was very profitable business for Scanlon and his company.

Set goals for personal self-improvement. Once each year you should take a personal inventory to analyze your own strengths and weaknesses. Take a blank sheet of typing paper and draw a line down the center. On one side write down your strengths and on the other side list your weaknesses. After you have done that, determine which of your weaknesses you are going to tackle in the year ahead. I am not referring to New Years' resolutions which are soon forgotten when the bloom of champagne wears off. What I have in mind is a total commitment to eliminate at least one negative during the ensuing period.

Since this is an "IDEA" book, I suggest for openers that you consider one negative that seems to appear on every salesperson's evaluation sheet. I refer to a difficulty in recovering from sales lost and errors made. I know from personal experience that having a sale almost in the palm of your hand and then suddenly having something happen so the rug is pulled out from under you, can be devastating. I've been screwed, tatooed, and unglued out of several good contract jobs in my time in the field, and believe me, it took a lot of soul searching on my part to quit licking my wounds and tighten my belt to get ready for the next battle. Whenever I got socked good and hard on a job, I always remembered the admonition of one of my first managers: "Always follow this rule: if you make a mistake, don't worry about it; but if you repeat the same mistake, then it's time to begin worrying."

How do *you* react to lost sales and mistakes? This could well be an area for setting your own long term goal for personal improvement. Perhaps you have another thought concerning a goal for self improvement, but the important thing is that whatever your own goal is, get at it immediately!

Do you know what dollar volume you are shooting for during the year ahead? What are your prime targets for both established and new business for the upcoming twelve months? Have you decided to wash out at least one personal weakness as a step to increase your effectiveness as a salesperson? If you have taken positive steps in these three areas, you are building a solid foundation for your important short term plans.

How To Use Short Term Plans

Once your long terms goals have been established, their execution will depend in a large measure on how effectively you make and implement your short range plans. It makes no difference what your product is. The basic principles of good planning are applicable to all. It seems incredible that so many salespersons are so careless when it comes to making plans in their work. There are tens of thousands of people involved in selling knocking down salaries and commissions, who don't know the meaning of the word *plan*. They could do so much better for themselves if they would make a concerted effort to put planning in their work schedules.

Typical of this type of salesman was Bucky Bowers, salesman for a steel products distributor. His sales manager told the story, "Bucky was a young salesman with great potential, but he always seemed to be floundering and not putting out to the full extent of his capabilities. One day I asked him what he was doing concerning his long term and short term plans. I was somewhat dumbfounded when he leveled with me and said, 'Quite frankly, I leave the long term plans for you to decide. As for the so-called short range plans, I guess I just rock along and roll with the punches. Every day after breakfast I get in the car and begin to think about where I will go. I really don't make any plans in advance. Don't get me wrong, however. I work hard, always put in a full day, and make a lot of calls.'

"When I questioned him further as to how he planned for his individual calls, he replied, 'Oh, I just grab my old case and maybe a couple of samples of something new and walk into the customer's place of business. I always give the stock a quick look-see, and if there are any empty spots, I really bear down to get an order. Otherwise, I just sit around and talk. I'm on a friendly basis with all of my buyers and if they need anything, they'll order it from me.'

"Because of Bucky's honesty, I was determined to sell him on starting to plan his work. When I pointed out to him how he could accomplish more with less effort if he would quit spinning his wheels and put some purposeful planning in his work, he became a changed person. He started to make plans on a weekly, daily, as well as customer-to-customer basis. At the end of his first year of his new modus operandi, Bucky's commissions had increased 18%. His enthusiasm was such that at an early date he became the youngest assistant sales manager the company ever had. All because he was smart enough to recognize the importance of planning."

The Importance Of Elasticity In Planning

Your plans must be like tall buildings—well structured, but at the same time flexible enough to withstand strong winds and earthquakes. If your plans are rigid and have no provision for modifications and alterations to cope with changes in circumstances, then you are tying your own hands behind your back. If you adopt an attitude of, "I'll stick with my plan come hell or high water," you won't be able to roll with the punches and you'll set up your own roadblocks on the road to successful selling.

Take a lesson from a football coach. You have no doubt watched a football game and have witnessed coaches and their assistants on the sidelines wearing headsets, talking with others who have clipboards, and making notes as the game progresses. Up in the stands are the scouts, who are carefully watching for any weaknesses in the defense of the opposing team. The game plan may have called for a concentration of plays up the center, but when it is discovered that the opponent's defense is jamming the middle of the line and is stopping the offense cold—what happens? Does the coach adopt the attitude that he has made his game plan and won't change it? If he is rigid and sticks to his "up the middle" plan, refusing to make adjustments, he'll probably lose the game. If he has flexibility, as all good coaches have, he will immediately make adjustments. He'll start to loosen up the opponent's defense by running end sweeps and calling for passes. The result—the defense can no longer concentrate on the center of the line, so the original game plan starts to work effectively.

Salespersons should take a lesson from a football coach who has a built in elasticity in his game plan. While it is imperative for a salesperson to have a "game plan" for each call he makes, he must be prepared to face up to the unexpected from his opponent, the buyer.

How one salesman profited from flexibility in planning. Henry Wintred was one of several successful insurance salesmen I have known throughout the years. He once told me of a selling experience that points up the consequence in having a built-in flexibility in making and working of plans. He had an appointment with the head of a fast growing company. As was his practice, he had developed a well-devised portfolio which on paper outlined his plan to sell this man personal life insurance. Henry told me that when he had reached the halfway point of his presentation, he sensed that his prospect was not one bit interested in his proposal, and that for him to go on would constitute a waste of time for both men.

At the proper moment, Henry shifted gears, and using his past experience and expertise, turned to the subject of group insurance for the company employees. His client immediately showed an interest. Henry was an expert in the use of the question and answer technique, and soon generated a lively conversation on the subject of group insurance, particularly as it pertained to his client's company requirements. He eventually sold a program that involved a much larger commission for himself than he would have realized from the sale of the individual policy.

Henry had planned well, but when he saw that he was on a dead-end street he shifted his presentation, and by being flexible got involved in discussing a program that turned out to be extremely worthwhile. That's why Henry Wintred was a winner. That's why he was a member of the Million Dollar Club.

Salespersons often tend to take the easy way out and find it difficult to face up to reality. The only way you can effectively implement a program of planning your work and then working your plan is to be prepared, look ahead, and when necessary, adjust to circumstances.

HOW TO WORK YOUR PLAN TO CREATE SALES

When you are about to begin working your plan you are getting down to the nitty-gritty of selling. You have reached the moment of truth—the point of no return. You have acquired product knowledge along with certain techniques and skills, and you have planned and planned. The day has arrived when you step into the arena with your adversary, armed with all the tools in your selling arsenal. Your opponent awaits you and you quickly discover that he also is well equipped—with resistance ordnance from his own arsenal. You face him, standing alone. What happens will depend in a large measure on how well you have done your home work.

Use Careful Thinking In Carrying Out Your Plans

In this book I have given you selling techniques that you can use when you start to work your plans. Somewhere among them you will find methods and skills that will help you face up to almost every type of situation.

Someone once said about the game of football, "Winning is 75% brains and 25% brawn. Many games are lost on confusion and carelessness, even when the loser has superior talent." I think the same can be said about selling. Salespersons often spend a lot of time making plans and then blow sales because they become careless in their execution. Selling is a thinking game and you have to be on your toes every minute you are in the arena with your buyer.

What do you do when your buyer says, "I'm very happy with the products I am handling and wouldn't want to make any changes right now." When you are faced with this "toughie," what do you say? It's time to reach for all of the skills that are available to you. Here are two suggested avenues that I have seen others use effectively:

1. By all means, don't knock your competitor. Agree with the buyer that he has been wise in selecting the line he is handling. Then, instead of talking merchandise, talk *merchandising*. Talk about profitability, turnover, stock control, etc.—anything to get him to open up. Maybe your competitor isn't knowledgeable in these areas. If your buyer admits to any weakensses in his setup, use your skills to show him what he can do to plug the leak in his dike. If you can find just one thing that touches a nerve, then you are on your way to helping him.

2. You might take the *exclusive* route. If you have products that have exclusive features that the line he is carrying doesn't have, hammer away at them. Forget your whole line. Just single out your exclusives and concentrate on them to try to get your foot in the door.

You Must Have Confidence In Your Plans

Unless you are sure of yourself and know that you have done a good job of preparation, you are going to run into trouble when you execute your plans. Always remember that planning alone won't get the order for you. You also have to have the know-how to use the tools in your arsenal to put those plans to work. Planning and working your plan—they are inseparable. You can count on one thing—if your plans aren't good and if you don't have confidence in them, you'll experience difficulty in trying to work them. Conversely, you can have perfect plans, but if you do not know how to properly execute them, you'll never grab the brass ring on the selling merry-go-round.

Put Your Selling Techniques And Skills To Work For You

Selling skills and techniques are available to all salespersons, but the trouble is they don't always use them.

I suggest that you set up and follow a two-step program. First—learn what these skills and techniques are. Second—consciously use them. Just knowing is not enough. You have to knowingly use them if they're going to help you talk your way to successful selling. What good are knowledge and know-how if you don't put them to work?

I have been astounded at the number of salespersons who use many of the skills and techniques we have discussed throughout the pages of this book without having an awareness of what they are doing. They don't realize when they are applying a specific technique to a given situation. How much more effective if they were to use these techniques *deliberately* to spearhead their sales presentations!

It is quite probable that not all of the techniques we have mentioned are applicable to your business. On the other hand, there are some that I know can be useful and helpful to you. I suggest that you single out those that are pertinent and make a reminder list of them. Then use them at every opportunity—until they become as vital a part of your selling program as your product knowledge and know-how.

Once you have finally sharpened your skills and techniques, then, and only then, will you be able to do an effective job in talking your way to successful selling. Include the selling techniques and skills in your long range and short range plans—then use them when you work your plans.

10

HOW TO KEEP THE BUYER FROM SAYING "NO"

It has often been said that selling begins when the buyer says "no." I disagree. When the buyer says "no" and really means it, that's usually the time when selling stops. This may be another contrary opinion, but I contend that good salesmanship is talking your way to the sale with "preventive medicine" ideas and techniques that keep the buyer from reaching the point where he says "no." The secret is to button things up before he has a chance to reach into his arsenal and pull out his big weapon on you.

Experienced salespersons can usually tell when they are "coming through" to the buyer. You should be able to recognize that "roadblock" where the buyer begins to falter and back off. When that happens, timing becomes an extremely important factor. You have to know when to reach into your own arsenal for weapons that will help you consummate the sale before the buyer strikes you out with his "no" ball. Depending upon circumstances, there are a number of techniques you can employ to that end. They are all time tested, and they can work for you as they have worked for others.

HOW THE SUCCESS STORY TECHNIQUE CAN LEAD TO SUCCESSFUL SALES

The success story technique is one of the most useful selling skills available to salespersons because it has such a universal application. The effective use of this technique is based on the premise that what is good and works for one customer, will be good and work for another. Buyers are always receptive to hearing about the successes of others in their business. That's one way they learn what to do and what not to do.

Let Your Buyers Know What Others Are Doing

One sure way to pique the interest of a customer is to relate to him what others in a situation similar to his are doing. That is why the success story technique is so effective. It can be used to completely transform the mood of your buyer from one of disinterest to one of curiosity. Everyone wants to know what the other guy is doing—your buyers are no exception.

Tom Lamberts, a star wholesaler floor covering salesman replied, in answer to a question concerning what he attributed his success to, "Briefly stated—using the success of one customer to help me sell another. I wasn't doing too well until I stumbled onto this technique in selling. First you take each one of your customers and find out who their friends in the business are and which dealers in other communities they respect. That's the hard part! Then you put your information to work. For example, only this morning I was showing a new line to Simpson of Royal Floors. He wasn't too receptive—said he had no open to buy and was loaded with stock; you know—the usual song! Then I told him that his good friend Randall over in Westgate had bought a roll of each of the new patterns just the day before. Simpson immediately became interested and his whole attitude changed. If Randall bought it, it must be good."

Lamberts reached into his sales case, pulled out his order pad and continued, "Look, to prove my point—here is the order Simpson gave me. He bought a roll of each pattern after I told him Randall had ordered them. And mind you, he was about to turn me down, until I mentioned Randall. If a salesman doesn't use this kind of information about his dealers to help him sell, he's out of his mind." Just to prove that Tom Lamberts wasn't crazy, his commission for the year just ending amounted to better than $27,000.

Use Your Key Accounts To Help You Get Sales

Every territory has *key accounts*. These are the bellwethers, the people who set the pace of activity. They are the successful merchants—the ones all others look up to and try to emulate. You know who they are and so do all of the rest of your customers. The important question is—are you smart enough to use their successes to help you sell your other dealers?

Rod Kurlen, a factory representative handling several lines of sportswear, used the success story technique to increase his sales. He was doing only an average job as a salesman until he decided to put his key accounts to work for him. He established a practice of first selling his key accounts any new items to "market test" them before hitting his whole territory. Then, if they moved successfully, he had ammunition to take to his other dealers.

He said, "The smaller operators want to know what the big boys are doing. When I tell them that Luxury Clothing, Moderne

Haberdashers, Stylist Shop and others bought a given item and have already reordered, sales resistance weakens and I write a lot of nice business. I guess it's a matter of prestige or ego. I don't know, but whatever it is, using the successes of my key accounts has certainly put more dough in my pockets. I increased my commissions $3,500 the first year."

HOW THE TWIST TECHNIQUE CAN HELP YOU TALK YOUR WAY TO SUCCESSFUL SELLING

At one time I had the occasion to negotiate a lease with Morton Mitchel, a realtor in a large metropolitan area to which I had been transferred. He had a modest office and seemed to be doing fairly well, but it was obvious that he wasn't tearing the world apart.

About eight years later, I bumped into Mitchel one night at the theatre. Everyone was in a hurry, so he handed me his card and suggested we have lunch together the following day. I was delighted to join him. Quite a change had taken place in those eight years. He occupied a beautiful new modern office, and "success" seemed to be written on its walls. I couldn't resist the temptation to get nosey, so I asked, "Mort, what has happened since I last saw you? You have really blossomed out. What's your secret?"

He smiled and responded, "The twist, my friend—that's what did it for me."

I asked, "Just what do you mean by that?" It was the first time I was to hear about the *twist technique* and how using it was making money for Mitchel.

He continued, "Not long after I first met you, I decided to do something about improving my business. One day I was showing a house to a young couple. The owner was there and trotted along. Every time the clients raised an objection, the owner got her back up and argued. She finally drove them out of the house with her caustic tongue.

That night the twist idea suddenly came to me. I decided first of all that in the future I would make it a policy to never show a house while the owner was present. Secondly, I would never take a prospective client into a house without having first studied it carefully so I could anticipate any objections that might be brought up. I would take a general contractor with me to give estimates on what certain obviously necessary alterations would cost a new buyer."

"Where does the twist technique come in?" I asked.

"Oh—the twist is agreeing with the customers on everything they say, including their objections. It worked the very first time I tried it. I took a couple into a large house. When the wife remarked that the fireplace was 'just awful', I agreed with her and suggested that for only $500 certain changes, which I showed her, could be made to modernize it. Every time they objected to something I agreed, and then told them what could be done to overcome their objection and approximately how much it would cost to do it. I went all over the house agreeing with every objection they made—and I sold the house! The twist is standard procedure for everyone in my office now. Never argue—always agree when they object! I tell you, it works every time."

The twist technique certainly worked for Morton Mitchel. Based on what he told me, he "twisted" his way to $125,000 that year.

Every salesperson can put this technique to good use. Basically, the twist technique is the skill of taking a buyer's objection and turning it into a positive selling point. Morton Mitchel did it—so can you!

HOW TO USE THE SWITCH TECHNIQUE TO TALK YOUR WAY TO SALES

Actually, there are three basic applications of the *switch technique*. I consider only the third one to be good salesmanship.

You'll Never Win By Baiting and Switching

First, there is the "bait and switch" tactic that is sometimes used in unscrupulous advertising and selling. The buyer is lured into a store by an enticing ad. On examination of the merchandise, however, it either falls short of what it was purported to be, or the customer is greeted with, "Very sorry—we're all sold out." In either case, an effort is then made by the seller to switch the buyer to something else. "This costs more, but it is a much better value, etc." Bait and switch! That is definitely not what I refer to in this chapter!

The Pressure Switch Doesn't Always Work

Then there is the "pressure switch" tactic. This is sometimes used in selling automobiles, insurance, and real estate, just to name a few businesses. When the salesperson isn't making points with the buyer, he suddenly backs off on one pretense or another and a high pressure artist, the "closer," takes over. Then the heat begins. Any time they switch salespersons on you, brace yourself, because the boom is about to be lowered on you. Perhaps this tactic works with some people, but it is definitely not the type of switch I am referring to in this chapter.

The Product Switch Can Increase Your Sales

A well prepared salesperson is like a stud poker player. You don't expose your whole hand on the first go around—you always keep that card in the hole well covered. Despite all of your care in planning, you sometimes select the wrong thing to sell the buyer. When his interest starts to wane, then you have to think in terms of showing your hole card—switching to something else. In order to effectively use the switch technique you must be so well coordinated in your planning that you are prepared to change to another product if your buyer is giving a negative reception to your first choice. Timing and flexibility become two important factors.

Just as a football coach knows when to put a substitute on the field, so must you have an awareness of the time to make your switch. Unlike the "bait and switch" tactic and the "pressure switch" mentioned earlier, the true switch, the product switch, effectively used, is a mark of good salesmanship.

Call your own "audibles." You have no doubt watched a football game and have observed a smart quarterback change a play sent in from the bench by calling an audible. He apparently saw something in the defensive alignment that prompted him to make the change. A sharp salesperson, likewise, can call his own "audible" when he detects something in his conversation with the buyer that tells him to switch.

Richard Tabler, an account executive for an investment house, was an expert in the use of the switch technique. He used his knowledge of tax free municipal bonds to open the door to new clients and once he had an opportunity to study their investment portfolios, he would switch to other types of investments. In his own words Richard said, "You've got to be on your toes and do a lot of thinking to stay ahead of your competitors in this business. Whenever I start out with a new client, I use municipal bonds as my wedge to open the conversation. I have made quite a study of them and think I have most of the answers concerning them. I use this knowledge to turn the conversation to other investments. Actually I don't sell an awful lot of muni bonds, but they sure do help me to switch to other bonds or stocks and achieve my main purpose—to open new accounts." That Richard succeeded is best shown by the fact that he was consistently in the $50,000 a year income bracket. Using the switch technique made a handsome living for him!

Every salesperson can use the "audible" system to advantage, provided he has done a good job of planning. Again, product knowledge and know-how become the keys as to how effectively it works. Like the quarterback who calls an audible and goes for a TD when he sees a weak spot in the defense, so you can go for the order by putting to use the switch technique—the product switch.

HOW TO USE THE BEST SELLER TECHNIQUE TO TALK YOUR WAY TO SALES

Manufacturers are constantly vying with each other to gain the lead in styling, pattern, color, and design. As a result, great emphasis is placed on research and design, and large amounts of money are spent on both in the race to get ahead of competition. As one eminent industrialist commented several years ago, "In today's economy, you've got to run like hell to stand still!" That just about sums up the whole competitive picture. New products are constantly being added, but with each one there are certain risks involved. The word from "upstairs" is—will it sell? That's the big question mark as manufacturers roll dice on the merchandising crap table.

Don't Overlook Your Winners

Salespersons for the most part are quick to scramble for business on "the new stuff" and tend to overlook the old reliables—their products that have proven themselves in the marketplace. These are the best sellers—the top of the line. If you don't know what your best sellers are, you are missing the boat. Knowing them and using them in your selling efforts can mean the difference between success or failure for you.

Willis Reading, representative for a wholesale drug supply company, learned to use his best sellers to increase his business. It wasn't until he started to check his records at the beginning of each year to determine where he was getting his business that he learned that over 50% of his dollar volume was coming from only 10% of his products. He singled out the 10%—his best sellers—and developed a portfolio showing pictures and containing pertinent information on each item. He carried it with him on every call and used it as a "check-off sheet" with his buyers. He also used it to pinpoint certain products for setting up segregated desplays.

Reading was so adamant in his emphasis on having his customers stock his best sellers that he was soon nicknamed "Old Best Seller". He didn't mind at all—just so they bought from him! Which they apparently did because he increased his business 20% the first year he started to carry his best seller portfolio.

It is only natural that alert merchants are always looking for new and exciting products. Be sure to get your share of this business, but at the same time remember that your bread and butter items are your best sellers. Don't desert your old friends—they can do a lot for you.

Always Keep Your Best Seller List Updated

The pressure in the marketplace for new products and designs can cause things to do a rapid turnabout. Some of today's best sellers can be on your drop list two years from now. New materials and other innovations can alter the composition of your best seller list from one year to the next. It therefore becomes imperative that you take a look at your list each year and update it by removing items that have run their course and inserting the lively, in-heavy-demand products.

At the beginning of each year Joe Ellerson, who sold kitchen supplies, compiled his new list of best sellers and had small cards printed, listing them and showing current prices. He gave these cards to his customers to keep them informed as to which of the items he carried were moving the best.

When asked if it was worth the trouble to make up the cards, he replied, "It sure is! You know, your best sellers change every year.

New products replace old ones that have fallen by the wayside. Just having the cards to give to my buyers provides me with another opportunity to talk about my best sellers with them. Over the years I have been surprised at what these cards really do. The buyers like them and I know they help my business."

Perhaps your line is such that having cards printed would not be practical for you. I do strongly urge you, however, to have an awareness of the ever changing trends that make it necessary for you to stay on top of your best sellers. They are your money makers, so keep them current and let your buyers know what they are.

HOW THE VALUE VS. PRICE APPROACH CAN PRODUCE SALES FOR YOU

What do you do when your buyer reaches into his arsenal and pulls out this weapon on you: "Your prices are too high!"

This is a common tactic often employed by buyers who have reached the point where they are about to say "no." There is bound to be someone whose prices are cheaper than yours, so don't fall for that old saw. It only gives you an opportunity to keep the conversation moving by talking profit to your buyer—after all, that is the one thing he is most interested in.

Talk Turnover vs. Price To Make Sales

Any businessman will tell you that unless you have good turnover it is impossible to run a profitable operation. When your dealer tells you that your prices are too high, ask him if he's willing to sacrifice turnover just to save a few dollars on cost. Quality, style, color, design—these are what create turnover; not cost or price. Remind him that it's not what he *pays* for a product, but what he can *sell* it for that determines its profitability.

Joe Boarder, a sales representative for a dry goods distributor, told a friend, "My products are always high compared with my competitors. If all buying was done on strictly a price basis, I'd have a time of it getting any business. I tell my dealers to forget about price and think value—concentrate on what they can sell it for, not how much it costs. I constantly remind them that nothing is cheap if it won't sell, and that only those items that have value in good quality, style, and design will give them the turnover that will insure a profit for them. When they throw that price bit at me, I simply tell them that I am selling value—quality products at a reasonable price. You naturally have to tell them what your stuff costs, but I never get involved in a price comparison hassle. I only talk about price as it relates to value, turnover and profit."

Boarder must have been on the right track because his commissions average better than $2,000 a month.

Bargain Hunters Never Win

There are so many people who are constantly looking for bargains.

All they are interested in is price—nothing else seems to matter. Women will spend hours driving from one market to another to save a few cents on individual items, not realizing that the cost of gasoline and wear and tear on their car more than offsets any savings on their groceries. People will sacrifice quality on a set of automobile tires to save a few dollars, only to have trouble with them from the day they are installed.

The cheapest isn't always the cheapest. Quite often it turns out that the most expensive is the cheapest in the long run. Some of your customers are "taken in" by price. Just show them something that has been discontinued and has been discounted 20% and they'll snap it up, not stopping to ask themselves if it will sell for them. They only have eyes for the price tag. You can usually spot this kind of buyer because his stock is full of "dogs" that don't sell.

It's risky enough for a merchant to buy something with any assurance that it will sell, but when he deliberately sets out to buy price, turnover goes out of the window. He doesn't buy value, and without value he can't possibly make a profit.

HOW THE SQUEEZE PLAY TECHNIQUE CAN PRODUCE SALES

One thing most selling techniques have in common is that they have an appeal to human nature. The *squeeze play technique* works because it appeals to man's greed. Just tell someone they can't have or do something and you immediately trigger a desire.

How A Dress Saleslady Used The Squeeze Play Technique

Effie was a saleslady in an exclusive dress section of a large department store. She had a loyal following because she took special precaution to make certain that no two of her customers would ever run into one another wearing the same dress. Effie was clever. When she wanted to divert a customer's interest from a dress, she would put another dress on the rack and remark, "This one is beautiful—I am holding it for Mrs. Smythe, she's just your size." Naturally, *that* dress was immediately wanted by her customer! When she persisted, Effie would say, "Well, I haven't heard from Mrs. Smythe for a couple of days. Perhaps just this once I'll take a chance—you can have it."

How A Stamp Dealer Sold Stamps Using The Squeeze Technique

I can personally attest to the effectiveness of the squeeze play technique because several times I was victimized by a stamp dealer from whom I purchased stamps when I had an interest in collecting them. It seemed that every time I was in his store and saw a stamp I really wanted but couldn't make up my mind to buy because of its cost, he would warn me, "I have a customer coming in this afternoon who is very much interested in that stamp—you better take it."

Nine times out of ten I did take the stamp. I just wasn't about to let the other guy have it! Then, after I left the store with stamp in hand, I would start to wonder. Was there actually another customer who wanted that stamp or was he giving me a snow job? However, twice when I left to "think it over," I returned the next day only to learn that the stamp was gone. Then he would say, "Like I told you; I had another customer who wanted it. Too bad you couldn't make up your mind!"

I was never sure about that dealer, but he certainly did sell me some expensive stamps using the squeeze play technique. It is a very effective technique but I caution you that when you use it, be sure there actually is another customer. Use it honestly—otherwise you might get caught with your hand in the cookie jar and not only lose a sale, but a customer as well.

HOW TO USE THE DIVERSION TECHNIQUE TO TALK YOUR WAY TO A SUCCESSFUL SALE

This is a "detour" tactic that can work for you when your buyer starts to clam up or stall on you. You can always tell when he reaches a point where his interest is about to fade away, and if you don't pull something out of your arsenal, you're going to lose him! The purpose of this technique is to throw your buyer off guard by making a temporary departure from your sales pitch to give yourself a breather. It also gives him something else to think about and brings him into the conversation—it makes him talk! Salespersons often get themselves so involved in what they are selling, they have a tendency to overlook this very effective selling technique. When the buyer starts to send out negative waves, it is time to act quickly by changing the subject so he will be put in a positive frame of mind.

How One Salesman Used The Detour Technique

Matt Turner was a bed and mattress salesman who was an expert in using the *diversion technique*. When he was trying to break into an account and ran into stiff buyer resistance, his "detour" tactic was to suggest that the buyer hold a sidewalk or parking lot sale to divest himself of dead inventory. He would submit a preplanned program, tailored to the individual buyer's requirements. Few buyers could resist an opportunity to move out stagnated items, including, of course, shopworn mattresses, which gave Matt an opportunity to discuss replacement with fresh new stock.

Matt once said, "I have yet to run across a buyer who isn't interested in getting rid of dead stock that has good money tied up. They will always listen to any ideas. I usually suggest they mark their items down to just below cost to get rid of them. You can be sure that on the day a sale is held, little old Matt is right there with order book in hand to help the buyer select new stock. It has worked very well for me and helps me achieve a maximum bonus of 20% every year. One of the largest orders I ever wrote was late one Saturday night following a customer's parking lot sale. He really cleaned house!"

How A Saleslady Used The Diversion Technique To Advantage

If you are a salesman, stop for one moment and put yourself in the position of the first woman to ever hit a territory carrying a line of merchandise. The first one I ever met was Sally Donner, a very sharp and knowledgeable salesperson, representing a furniture manufacturer. She met with only reasonable success when she started out, spending much of her time explaining her company's new policy to hire women for field sales work. When the buyers became accustomed to her and accepted her, she began to work on ways to improve her volume. She concluded that what was needed was something to divert her buyers' attention from what she was selling when they lost interest. She decided to set herself up as an expert on interior decorating. Sally had a basic knowledge of fabrics and color, and worked out color schemes for each item of furniture she handled. She carried samples of carpets, vinyls, wallpaper, and paint color swatches. She used the diversion technique to get her buyer to concentrate on the materials that could be used to enhance the appearance of her furniture items. While her competitors were using the quality approach, hers was the decorative approach.

The first year Sally started her program, she increased her commissions 19%. Sally explained, "If you want to sell anything—I don't care what it is—wrap it up in a pretty package and put a big ribbon on it. The more attractive the box, the better it will sell. That's why my furniture sells. I tie a big red bow on it!"

HOW TO BENEFIT FROM THE BOW-OUT TECHNIQUE

You may wonder why I am suggesting that picking up and leaving without an order is a kind of technique, when the real purpose of selling is to get the order. I call this the *tactical retreat technique*. After you have pulled out all stops, without results, and you feel that the buyer is going to turn you down, it is sometimes wise to beat him to the punch by backing away. The very moment you know your have lost the order is the time to start thinking about how to derive some kind of positive benefit from your call on the buyer. Of course, if you are convinced that selling starts when the buyer says "no," you may want to persist and continue to push for the order. Perhaps you will, on occasion, be successful in talking your way to the sale, but if you aren't, you walk out with no order in hand and no benefit whatever from your contact with the customer. In fact, your pressure may have been harmful to your future relations with the buyer.

Proper timing and use of the bow-out technique will provide you with these benefits:

1. *You set the stage for the next call on the buyer.* He feels that he isn't being high pressured, so the welcome mat will be out on your next call. At all costs you have to avoid giving him the impression that you are turning the heat on him, so before you reach that point, bow-out and call it a day.
2. *It gives you time to think.* Perhaps you fouled up somewhere in your presentation. I think it is important that you recognize the fact that you cannot and do not always put out your best effort. Perhaps you may not feel well and should have stayed in bed that morning, but being conscientious, you get up and make your calls. You can't possibly give your best under such circumstances. By using the bow-out technique you have a chance to think about how you can improve on your pitch so you will be better prepared on your next call, when you are feeling better.
3. *It gives your buyer time to think.* Herb Pearson, an automobile salesman was calling on a buyer who controlled a large fleet of cars. New models had just come out and he was anxious to nail down the business. In the course of his presentation, he suddenly sensed that the buyer had something else on his mind, perhaps a personal problem, so he bowed out. Pearson was not surprised when he returned to his office later that day to learn that the buyer had telephoned him, requesting that he return the following morning. He did, and made the sale which gave him a commission of $1,600. If he had persisted on his first call, he would have lost the order. In fact, the buyer told him exactly that! Because he bowed out and gave the buyer time to think, Pearson got the order.

Lest I be misunderstood, let me make it clear that I abhor any salesperson who is not willing to stand up and fight for an order, but at the same time admire him when he is smart enough to realize that he can achieve a more positive benefit by backing off and waiting for the next time. Always have a consciousness of this technique and put it to good use when you are talking your way to sales—you may surprise yourself. Follow this **rule**: always make sure to derive some positive benefit from your sales effort, even though you don't write an order.

11

TALK YOUR WAY TO SUCCESSFUL SALES BY ASKING FOR THE ORDER

In the final analysis, salesmanship boils down to one simple fact—you have to ask for the order if you expect to get the business. If you don't, your product knowledge, preparation, presentation and persuasion, along with your selling skills and techniques, will be meaningless. You can count on one thing for sure. The buyer, whether it's in insurance, monkey wrenches, brassieres, nose drops, or whatever, isn't going to get down on his kees and plead with you to pull out that order book.

In that every-present jousting bout with the buyer, one of his secret weapons is that too often the salesperson will either chicken out, goof up, or simply not know when and how to ask for the order. When this happens, the salesperson may make a friend out of the buyer, but it certainly isn't conducive to winning business. He walks out with no order in hand, but with the buyer very pleased with himself and thinking, "There goes a real nice guy."

Be honest with yourself and take a good look at your own track record. How many times has that happened to you? Actually, it has occurred too many times to innumerable salespersons. You can count on this—you won't achieve 100% success in your sales efforts just because you ask for the orders—but you are buying yourself 100% failure if you don't!

WHY SALESPERSONS OFTEN FREEZE UP AT ORDER ASKING TIME

Perhaps some may feel that this topic should be covered by a psychologist. I prefer to believe that only one who has had years of practical experience in the marketplace, and has observed salespersons in diversified activities under all kind of circumstances, is best equipped to handle it. This is an extremely important subject, because it touches on one of the two "roadblocks" mentioned in Chapter 2.

It is disconcerting—yes, sometimes frightening—to see a salesperson with know-how and good product knowledge step into the arena with a buyer fully prepared, give a fine presentation, and then at the crucial moment, blow the sale. Most salespersons will admit that closing the sale is their weakest area. Why? It doesn't have to be!

Fear Of Failure—Fear Of Losing The Sale

One thing a baseball player fears more than anything else is a batting slump. He knows that once he hits a slump he becomes enmeshed in a losing syndrome from which it is seemingly impossible to extricate himself. Twenty times at bat and not one hit! He tries everything and is really bleeding inside—but still no hits! Then, he gets a hit—then another, and his confidence returns. The fear is gone and he's back on the stick again.

Salespersons likewise fear a selling slump. Suddenly, without explanation, nothing seems to go right. Buyers don't buy and orders are hard to come by. You try hard—but nothing seems to work for you.

Cotton Pearson, a very successful appliance salesman explained, "Once I went a whole week without scratching my order book. I damned near lost my mind—couldn't do anything right. I finally went to my boss and told him I was coming unglued. He suggested to me, 'Cotton, take a week off and go fishing. What you need is a good mental catharsis—you're full of fears. You're a good salesman, but you can't sell as long as you have a fear of failure.' I did what he suggested and finally got myself straightened out."

I pose a simple question. What is there to be afraid of? Most buyers are nice persons and are sympathetic. As a matter of fact, if you have made a well planned presentation, your buyer expects you to ask for the order. This is so important that I am repeating and italicizing it so you won't forget: *your buyer expects you to ask for the order*! Always remember that, when the spectre of fear begins to rear its ugly head. Just do your job well—you'll get the orders!

Fear Of Offending The Buyer

When you get to the point of asking for the order and you are afraid that you might antagonize or offend the buyer, chances are good that you entered the arena unprepared and are not sure of yourself. Somewhere along the line you are short on either product knowledge, preparation, presentation, or persuasion. Or can it possibly be that you are just plain stupid—like I was once, early in my selling career, when I didn't know better!

I was working a territory calling on furniture stores with a promotion on a line of inexpensive printed rugs. I stopped at one store where I hoped to pick up a nice order. The dealer was a pleasant individual and when I showed him my color plates, he agreed that the patterns were nice. However, business hadn't been too good and he didn't want to add to his stock. I didn't wish to offend him, so I picked up my lithographs and put them back in my case. I did not ask for an order!

He invited me back to his office for a cup of coffee and we had a nice time talking about fishing. Suddenly the front door opened and Johnson, one of my competitors, strolled down the aisle, loaded with samples.

My good friend, the buyer, said, "Here comes that Johnson guy. I'll get rid of him in a hurry. Don't go away." He walked out to where Johnson was standing.

When he returned, about ten minutes later, he smiled and said, "Well, I got rid of him." He then placed an order form on the top of his desk. Now any salesman worth his salt knows how to read upside down, so when I looked at that piece of paper, I quickly saw that my competitor had written an order for a dozen rugs! *He* was selling and *I* was sitting there like a dumb-dumb because I hadn't asked for the order myself! I was entertaining the buyer while Johnson was selling him.

I learned a hard lesson that afternoon. Need I say more?

Fear That The Presentation Has Not Been Good

If you expect to get an order every time you step into the arena with a buyer you are dreaming the impossible dream. One hard fact of selling is that you can't win them all! You older experienced salespersons understand this becuase you have taken your raps along with the good things that go with selling. If your expectations aren't realistic, you're in for a lot of disappointments and heartbreaks.

Salespersons often fail to realize that no two days are alike. Yesterday you felt like a million dollars and everything went smoothly. Today you have a headache, your nose is running, and nothing seems to be going right. Perhaps you have received bad news and you are all shook up. How you feel can have a direct bearing on the results you attain.

As I suggested in Chapter Ten, when you know you're not coming through to the buyer, bow-out and come back at a later date. Don't let fears get hold of you—everyone has his off days. Tomorrow is another day—just hold onto the thought that things will be better!

Fear That You Have Been Outsmarted By The Buyer

You have to stay on the offensive from the very moment that you step into the arena with the buyer, until you ask for the order. You have the ball from the beginning. Once you lose it, however, and your buyer puts you on the defensive, your chances of asking for the order and getting it are very slim.

It is always well to remember that may buyers were once salespersons themselves, so they know how to sell. They know all of the techniques and skills that are available to you, and they will not hesitate to use them—if you let them. In addition, they have their own private harassment techniques designed to make your life miserable.

I have seen a smart buyer get a salesperson so confused during a presentation that the latter was glad to get out—with or without an order. Confusion is one of the powerful weapons in the buyer's arsenal. If you entertain fears concerning what your buyer will do, he will quickly get your message. Don't let him put you on the run. Always keep control of the situation—stay a couple of jumps ahead of him. Stay with your game plan, regardless of what he says or does. If you do that, there is no way that he can outsmart you—unless, of course, you haven't come to the arena properly prepared.

THE IMPORTANCE OF TIMING IN ASKING FOR THE ORDER

Why is it that some salespersons are consistently successful at order asking time while many others fall down at this critical point?

There may be other valid reasons for this, but I have found that one thing that distinguishes a top salesperson from all others is an ability to know at exactly what point he should ask for the order. You can have all of the ingredients necessary for good salesmanship, but if you don't know *how* and *when* to ask for the order, you won't make it to the winner's circle. Good timing can mean the difference between success or failure for you.

The Gun Jumpers

At one end of the timing spectrum are the nervous Nellies and the eager beavers who can't resist pulling out the order book before they are finished with their sales pitch. Their timing is completely off. The quickest way to cool off a buyer is to ask for an order before you have completed your presentation—before you have made the sale! Your sales pitch certainly can't be very convincing if you stop right in the middle of it and ask for an order. The buyer wants to be sold, not prodded into buying!

Jerry Turner was an automobile salesman. He knew his product from A to Z and for the most part gave a good presentation. However, customers made him nervous—primarily because they were unpredictable, as all customers are. The minute a prospect was undecided and showed signs of getting ready to walk out, Turner all but lifted him bodily into his small office to try to get a signature on the dotted line. Actually, he was not a high pressure salesman—his timer just wasn't functioning properly. The inevitable result was that he invariably jumped the gun in trying to force his sales. Instead of selling his customers, he irritated them.

His manager finally had to take Turner off the sales force and put him in the service department. As a consequence, he suffered a loss in income of over $3,000 a year.

I urge you to make a self-analysis of how you react at order asking time. If you feel that you are a little edgy, slow down and try to summarize your presentation before you ask your buyer for the order. Two or three minutes can mean the difference between making or losing the sale.

The Stallers

At the opposite end of the spectrum are the stallers—the procrastinators—those who don't seem to be able to make up their minds when to ask for the order. You have all seen speakers lose their audience because of poor timing—not knowing when to sign off. The staller, likewise, loses sales because of poor timing in asking for the order.

I have found one thing to be true—you usually get only one chance to ask for the order! If you muff it, you miss the sale. The staller passes the point of no return without realizing what is happening. When he finally awakens to the fact that he has gone past order asking time, it is too late—he has already closed the door on the order.

The stallers are usually guilty of talking too much. They fail to pause to listen and watch for buying signals that tell them when it is time to ask for the order. (See Chapter 7)

If you feel that you may be a staller, I suggest that for the time being you make a concerted effort to try to shorten your sales presentations and that you carefully avoid any prolonged discussions. Don't talk your way out of an order by talking too much! Let your buyer do the talking—let *him* talk your way to an order.

The Synchronizers

These are the stars of the selling game—those who keep their selling motors so well tuned up that they know the exact moment to ask for the order. Some may say that they are endowed with a sixth sense—something most salespersons lack. Perhaps there is some truth in this, but I hold a contrary opinion. I believe that any salesperson can become a synchronizer if he works at it!

Just be sure that the cogs in your selling machine are always well lubricated and properly synchronized. You can do this if you will but use the simple common sense principles of selling that are found throughout the pages of this book. When you have everything in perfect working order, then you will know *when* and *how* to ask for the order. The stars of the game do—so can you, if you set your mind to it.

USING THE RIFLE VS. SHOTGUN APPROACH TO ASK FOR THE ORDER

A number of years ago two restauranteurs decided to open a large restaurant featuring only one main entre—prime ribs of beef.

Many people experienced in the business said it couldn't be done: the public wouldn't go for it; the gamble was much too risky. Just how wrong these critics were is best attested to by the large crowds in the lobby and cocktail bar waiting to get tables in this extremely popular restaurant.

The founders used the rifle approach to perfection. When you are finally seated at a table and the waitress joins you, she doesn't ask, "What will you have for dinner this evening?" What she says is, "How would you like your prime ribs this evening?" Just simple and powerful rifle selling. Not *what* do you want—but *how* do you want it!

I think many salespeople tend to scatter their shots. Instead of using the rifle approach as the two restaurateurs did, they use the shotgun approach. It is little wonder, therefore, that they experience difficulty in asking for the order. If you try to cover too much territory in your sales presentation, when you get down to the point of asking for the order you are faced with making a decision at the wrong time. The choice of what you are going to try to sell the buyer should come at the beginning, not the end, of the presentation. This is an important fact to remember!

How The Three-C Formula Works To Produce Sales

I was recently discussing the subject of rifle vs. shotgun selling with an old friend, Charles C. Chambers, who, although now drawing a pension and social security, was once a star performer for a dry goods house in both selling and sales management.

Chambers commented, "It's my opinion based on experience with salesmen that one of their basic weaknesses is that they don't always follow the script. By that I mean they don't take a direct approach to selling. They act as though they are in a sparring match with the buyer and spend most of their time in feeling him out. They don't get in any good solid blows. To help them avoid this, I developed a simple little formula that I called my *Three-C Method of Selling*: (1) choose, (2) concentrate, and (3) consummate."

"Those are your own initials!" I exclaimed.

He smiled and continued, "That's right—made it easy for the boys to remember. First you pick out and choose what you are going to sell the buyer; then you concentrate on it and give it the works, finally, you consummate it—you summarize and button up the sale by asking for the order. I found that if my men followed this formula, it kept them from vacillating and muddling up their presentation. You know, you don't carry a a shotgun when you're hunting big game—you use your rifle. Same's true in selling."

Using The Rifle Approach To Sell Suits

David Wisener, a salesman in a men's clothing store, at one time had control of what was in my wardrobe. Every time I went to him for a suit, he always started out by walking me down the rows of suits hanging on racks, listening for my comments. After our stroll, he seated me in a comfortable chair and excused himself. Within five minutes he would come back with never more than three suits. He watched me carefully and his eyes told him from the expression on my face which of the three I liked the most. He intuitively knew which one I was going to buy, so he rifled in on it. He scored a bullseye every time!

I used to josh him and once asked when I walked in, "Well, David—what kind of a suit are you going to con me into today?"

His reply was quick, "We'll walk down the racks. You keep on talking, and *when you tell me, I'll let you know!*"

David made $16,000 a year which in those days was good money. He learned early in his career that the more suits he showed, the more confused his customer became. The answer to selling suits was to show only two or three suits that he knew the customer would like—then zero in on the one that struck his buy nerve.

When you're selling, leave your shotgun at home and carry your rifle—unless of course, you're looking for birds.

MAKE YOUR OWN BREAKS FOR SUCCESSFUL SELLING

Abner Wilken had a nickname—he was called "Lucky" Wilken by his associates. It came about as a result of having knocked over one of the largest accounts in the state. For several years Wilken had faithfully called on Mr. Kerpen, owner of a chain of garden and home supply stores. Kerpen was an exclusive account with one of Wilken's competitors, but that didn't deter him from calling on him to feed him ideas on merchandising, turnover, mark-ups, stock control, etc.

Although Kerpen didn't buy from Wilken, he developed a high regard for this persistent and knowledgeable salesman. Then came a break! Kerpen had a complaint, and the competitor's salesman turned him down. A bitter argument ensued and as a result, other sources of irritation surfaced. Kerpen made a drastic decision. He decided to phase out the competitor's line and thenceforth would concentrate on Wilken's products. Lucky Wilken!

Was it just plain luck? I don't think so. To be sure, it was fortunate for him that Kerpen threw out his competitor, but the hard fact was that he had for years been setting the stage by building a strong position with this important buyer. He hung in there and made his own break. Lucky Wilken! Because of his perservance, he increased his income $4,200 a year just from sales to this one customer. Lucky Wilken!

When you get down in the dumps and begin to think that you're not getting any breaks out of life, remember that in most instances *you have to make your own breaks*—just like Wilken did.

I do believe, however, that you have to face up to this subject with realism. There is such a thing as luck. It is sometimes difficult to understand and explain some of the things that happen. You give the same pitch to two buyers—one buys, the other doesn't.

I am fully convinced that if you know all you can about your product, prepare yourself for a good presentation, and then use your powers of persuasion to get the order, the ball will bounce your way most of the time.

As one professional golfer said to another, "The more you know about this game, and the more you play and practice, the luckier you get!"

HOW TO USE PRE-REHEARSAL TO TALK YOUR WAY TO THE SALE

I am a firm believer in *practice selling*. It is just as important for a salesperson to practice using selling skills and techniques as it is for those big veteran linemen to constantly practice blocking and tackling. Practice helps them win games—it helps the salesperson win orders.

Sam Strickner, a hospital supply salesman, was an advocate of pre-rehearsal. He once said, "You're never too old to practice the fundamentals of selling, just as those baseball players are never so good that they don't spend a lot of time practicing in the batting cage. For my part, I always practice two things—the opening and the closing, with particular emphasis on the latter, when you ask for the order.

"It's good to work out things in advance before you see the buyer. In between calls, when I'm driving my car, I rehearse what I'm going to say on the next stop. It's a lot better than just sitting there and cussing out the traffic. Some of the things that pop up in my mind during those practice runs are directly responsible for my getting orders.

"Any salesman who doesn't do a lot of pre-rehearsing and practicing ought to go to a shrink to get his head examined."

Strickner said that the use of the *pre-rehearsal technique* helped him average in excess of $2,000 a month in commissions.

Perhaps you are one of those who contend that practice selling is somewhat elementary and is not for the experienced salesperson. All I can say is that if you believe that, your thinking battery is ready for a recharge. No salesperson is so good that he shouldn't devote as much time as he can to practice selling and pre-rehearsal. This is particularly true when it comes to order asking time.

Try to think of different ways that you can ask for the order, then test them in your actual calls on buyers. When you find something that works effectively, stay with it. Many successful salespersons will tell you that they have learned how and when to ask for the order through trial and error—a direct result of practice and pre-rehearsal.

A sales manager for an electronics firm once told me, "I wasn't too sold on practice until one of my younger salesmen showed me how wrong I was. I knew he was having a problem closing sales but attributed it to inexperience. In time, he would work his way out of it. He did just that—but much more quickly than I had ever hoped for.

"Jimmy made up his mind to strengthen his weak spot. He discussed the matter with his wife, and they set up a practice schedule. Alice was a sharp girl—she had had some experience in selling, so she was a capable "adversary" for her husband to work on. They both did such a fine job in their practice sessions that Jimmy's closing capabilities showed a marked improvement in a relatively short time. In fact, it was so noticeable that I asked him what he was doing.

"When he told me about his practice selling, I darned near flipped at first, but the more I thought about it the more I realized how sound his thinking was. You're not going to find many wives who can or will play "buyer" for their husbands, but I am convinced now that anyone in selling can practice on his own. All I can say is that it's worth the effort."

I agree. You have nothing to lose but much to gain if you set up for yourself a program of practice selling and pre-rehearsal. Practice at every opportunity—practice until it becomes a habit and then keep at it. Follow the admonition of a well-known pro football player—"When you think you have done enough practicing, that means you've got to do more."

HOW THE PRE-WRITTEN ORDER TECHNIQUE CAN BE EFFECTIVE FOR YOU

It may seem presumptuous to write an order in advance to hand to the buyer at the end of your sales pitch and expect it to stick. Making up pre-written orders is a sales technique that I have seen effectively used by some salespersons. While it does not have as broad an application as do some of the other techniques, I include it here because it pertains to the closing of the sale. It is just another way to ask for the order—and that's what this chapter is all about.

Howard Heyton, a wholesale household products salesman, used pre-written orders whenever his sources of supply came out with new products. Howard knew his territory well, and determined in advance what he thought each of his customers should buy.

He explained, "It simplifies things and saves a lot of time, too. I've had very few repercussions, although on occasion a buyer will cut down on the order. The important thing is that it's a great way to ask for the business—the old order book is automatically opened! It then boils down to a discussion of not *if* the buyer is going to buy, but *how much* he will buy. I only use the pre-written order on my new stuff—otherwise I stick to my regular selling program."

This technique helped Howard average $25,000 a year in commissions.

There may be times and circumstances when you can put the *pre-written order technique* to work for you. Only those who are experienced should use it, however, because improperly applied, it could backfire with serious consequences. When you set out to presume what the buyer should buy from you, you not only have to know your buyer, but you must know all about his business. Properly used, it can produce positive results for you.

TAKING THE BUYER'S VIEWPOINT WILL HELP YOU INCREASE YOUR SALES

Idealistically, it would be great if every time you entered the arena with the buyer he would listen patiently to your sales pitch, without ever interrupting you, and then at order asking time tell you he is ready and anxious to buy from you. Fortunately, it doesn't work out that way. If selling was that easy, there wouldn't be any need for salespersons.

Realistically, you very seldom enter the arena with the buyer and make your pitch without having him interrupt you and try to throw resistant roadblocks designed to keep you from asking for the order and getting it. That's the way it works out. That's why good salesmanship is so important—and so necessary.

When you take an objective look at selling, it all seems to boil down to whose viewpoint will prevail—yours or your buyer's. That's why it is imperative that you know what your buyer is thinking. Many salespersons make the mistake of concentrating on what *they* think instead of considering the buyer's point of view. It's, "I suggest—I believe—I want—I think." Most of the time the buyer isn't interested in your point of view and will respond positively only when you take the approach, "What do you suggest? What do you believe? What do you want? What do you think?"

In Chapter 1 I suggested the importance of classifying your buyers. Regardless of which category they fall in, they all have one thing in common—interest in their own point of view. Experienced salespersons understand this, and accommodate their selling program to their buyer's feelings. After all, when you ask the customer to buy something from you, you're talking about *his* money—not your own!

How One Salesperson Used The Turnabout Technique To Make Sales

Agnes McIntosh represented a stationers supply house. She had her own technique that she used just before order asking time to draw out an opinion from her buyer. She usually gave a capable presentation and then, at the crucial moment, stopped and said to the buyer, "If you were selling and I was the customer—which of these do you think would be best for me?"

Agnes always got an answer. It may not have been what she wanted to hear, but she always learned what the buyer was thinking—and that's what really counts at order asking time. Once she knew that, she was on her way to getting the order. Many times the buyer actually told her what he wanted to buy, so all that was left was the formality of opening the order book.

Agnes made $18,000 a year and attributed much of her success to using the *turnabout technique*. As she said, "It sure beats pounding a typewriter."

Magical Words To Use At Order Asking Time

There are certain words that always ring a bell with your buyer because they appeal to his point of view. Make it a habit to use them when possible.

1. I have already pointed out the importance of using the word *YOU*. When you use this, you bring the buyer into the conversation so instead of resisting you, he can actually help you make the sale.
2. And don't forget *PROFIT. Design your questions at order asking time to include this word. It has power, because it is the reason why your customer is in business.*
3. *VALUE* is another word that has a strong appeal to the buyer's point of view. He always wants to make sure that he is getting his money's worth.
4. *HELP* is a strong word when properly used. Always let your customer feel that you are there to help him.
5. *OPINION* is another word you should always remember and use. When you ask the buyer what his opinion is, you are adding air to his ego balloon.

There may be other words that are important, but I urge you to always keep these in mind: *you, profit, value, help* and *opinion*. They can work magic for you at order asking time.

USE THE POSITIVE APPROACH WHEN YOU ASK FOR THE ORDER

During the years I spent in the marketplace, I had an opportunity to "listen in" on many salespersons. The thing that interested me the most was how they made out at order asking time—what they said to try to induce the buyer to buy. It was always a pleasure to watch a salesperson talk his way to an order by knowing *how* to ask for it. Conversely, it was almost revolting to hear some of the things that were said at order asking time. You be your own judge as to which of the following approaches would most likely get orders for a salesperson selling shirts: (I add my own comments.)

1. "*How about some of these shirts, Mr. Smith*?" (unless he is low in stock, I question very much that he would buy.)
2. "*By the way, Mr. Smith—could you use a few of these shirts*?" (Such nonchalance! You can almost feel that the salesperson expects the buyer to turn him down.)
3. "*I wouldn't want you to miss out on these—they're really hot items*." (Wrong viewpoint! The buyer isn't interested in what you want!)
4. "*What's your opinion on these, Mr. Smith? Don't you think they are beautiful and would sweeten your stock*?" (A good, positive approach—much more likely to get results than the previous three.)
5. "*You wouldn't want to buy some of these shirts, would you, Mr. Smith*?" (Please don't laugh! I have actually heard so-called salespersons use this approach. This one is at the top of the no-no list.)
6. "*These shirts are priced right, Mr. Smith. How about putting some in your stock*?" (Only fair! Seems to lack punch to make the buyer want to buy.)
7. "*These shirts will add color to your stock, in addition to being profitable items. Here—let me help you select the patterns and sizes you will need*." (A strong positive approach. Buyer will find it difficult to turn this one down.)

8. "*These shirts are the best value we ever had, Mr. Smith. You'll be able to get a good markup on them*." (Also a good approach. It would be stronger if the salesperson offered his help in picking the colors and sizes.
9. "*Shall I send these now, or would you prefer that I wait until after the first of the month*?" (Bingo! An excellent positive approach. The salesperson assumes that the buyer is going to buy.)

Ask For The Order Believing You Will Get It

Many buyers find it difficult to make up their minds, even though they know that what you are trying to sell them is good for them. Unless you are positive in approach when you ask for the order, they will find justification in turning you down.

The only way you can take a positive approach is to honestly believe that you will make the sale. After all, if you don't believe that you'll get the order, why waste your time and the buyer's time going through the motions!

KEEP YOUR SELLING WHEEL ROLLING

On the first page of the introduction to this book I gave a definition of selling. I think it is fitting that this book begin and end with this definition, because selling is what it is all about.

Oversimplified, selling is taking a product or idea, developing a program for it, presenting it to a buyer who isn't necessarily interested in it, or doesn't think he wants it, or doesn't need it—and finally, TALKING HIM INTO BUYING IT, and making him feel happy that he did.

The four "P's" of selling are inexorably tied together. If you fail in one, it is a certainty that the others won't hold you up. I liken each of these to being a segment of a wheel that I call the *Selling Wheel*.

I use the symbol of the wheel to emphasize the interdependence and interrelationship of each. If one segment breaks down, the whole wheel cannot function properly. But, when you have good product knowledge, come into the arena well prepared, give a good presentation, use your know-how and persuasion, and know when and how to ask for the order, then your Selling Wheel will roll along to successful selling.

Keep your own Selling Wheel rolling. There are dollars at the end of the road.

INDEX

C

Q

R

S

T

OTHER BOOKS ON SELLING AND SALES MANAGEMENT FROM REWARD THAT YOU WON'T WANT TO MISS!

☐ 08015-0	**Boost Your Earnings in Real Estate,** Edward F. Rybka	$3.95
☐ 15741-2	**Complete Book of Model Business Letters,** Martha W. Cresci	$3.95
☐ 16751-0	**Confident Selling,** James R. Fisher, Jr.	$3.95
☐ 35483-7	**Getting Through to People,** Jesse S. Nirenberg	$3.95
☐ 40322-0	**How to Cash In on Your Hidden Memory Power,** William D. Hersey	$3.95
☐ 43528-9	**How to Talk Your Way to the Top,** Edward J. Hegarty	$3.45
☐ 44762-3	**The Human Side of Sales Management,** Burton Bigelow	$9.95
☐ 51622-9	**Kinesics: The Power of Silent Command,** Merlyn Cundiff	$3.95
☐ 51686-4	**Kuesel on Closing Sales,** Harry Kuesel	$3.95
☐ 53052-7	**Les Dane's Master Sales Guide,** Les Dane	$3.95
☐ 54531-9	**Magic Power Of Self-Image Psychology,** Maxwell Maltz	$3.95
☐ 54889-1	**The Management of Time,** James T. McCay	$3.95
☐ 57589-4	**Mental Dynamics: Power Thinking for Personal Success,** K. Thomas Finley	$2.95
☐ 60394-4	**Motivation and Persuasion in Real Estate Selling,** John E. Cyr	$5.95
☐ 68696-4	**Power With People,** James K. Van Fleet	$3.45
☐ 80420-3	**Sell Like an Ace — Live Like a King,** John H. Wolfe	$3.95
☐ 86043-7	**Successful Communication and Effective Speaking,** Millard Bennett and John [illegible] Corrigan	$3.95
☐ 87789-4	**Surefire Sales Closing Techniques,** Les Dane	$3.95
☐ 90689-1	**Tested Advertising Methods,** 4th Ed., John Caples	$3.95
☐ 91896-1	**36 Biggest Mistakes Salesmen Make and How to Correct Them,** George N. Kahn	$3.95
☐ 93495-0	**Twenty Steps to Power, Influence and Control Over People,** H. W. Gabriel	$3.95

Prices subject to change without notice.

BUY THEM AT YOUR LOCAL BOOKSTORE OR USE THIS HANDY COUPON

REWARD BOOKS — Dept. 4
Book Distribution Center
Route 59 at Brook Hill Drive
West Nyack, New York 10994

Please send me the books I have checked above. I am enclosing $__________ (please add 50¢ per copy to cover postage and handling). Send check or money order — no cash or C.O.D.'s. Please allow 4 weeks for delivery.

PLEASE PRINT OR TYPE

Mr. Mrs. Ms. Miss (circle one) Name ....

Address ....

City .... State .... Zip ....

Dept. 4 BP 6861(2)